MAKING SENSE OF
MATHEMATICS
FOR TEACHING

Grades 6–8

EDWARD C. NOLAN

JULI K. DIXON

GEORGE J. ROY

JANET B. ANDREASEN

Solution Tree | Press

a division of
Solution Tree

555 North Morton Street
Bloomington, IN 47404
800.733.6786 (toll free) / 812.336.7700
FAX: 812.336.7790

email: info@solution-tree.com
solution-tree.com

Visit **go.solution-tree.com/mathematics** to download the free reproducibles in this book.

Printed in the United States of America

Library of Congress Control Number: 2016932548

ISBN: 978-1-942496-45-8

Solution Tree
Jeffrey C. Jones, CEO
Edmund M. Ackerman, President

Solution Tree Press
President: Douglas M. Rife
Senior Acquisitions Editor: Amy Rubenstein
Managing Production Editor: Caroline Weiss
Senior Production Editor: Rachel Rosolina
Proofreader: Elisabeth Abrams
Text and Cover Designer: Abigail Bowen

Acknowledgments

Many thanks to my family, Michele and Calvin, for the wonderful support they continue to provide me in all of my endeavors. Many thanks to the Dixon Nolan Adams Mathematics associates who worked as a collaborative team in providing feedback on the content of this book. And finally, thanks to Jeff Jones, Douglas Rife, and Stefan Kohler from Solution Tree for helping us and believing in us and our vision for making sense of mathematics for teaching.

—Ed Nolan

My deepest love and gratitude to my daughters, Alex and Jessica, who continue to allow me to understand mathematics more deeply through their eyes, and to my husband, Marc, who supports me to spend countless hours doing so. I also wish to thank our author team—Ed, George, and Janet—for the wonderful collaborative environment they supported while writing this book.

—Juli Dixon

It is because of the encouragement of many individuals that I have realized a dream! To that point, I would like to thank "my girls," Tiffany and Izzy. My life is complete with you both! To my parents, you are my role models. Mom, I am constantly amazed at your faith. Dad, you may not be here to see this book, but your message to "never give up" is something that I live by. To Juli Dixon, Thomasenia Adams, and Ed Nolan, your vision and guidance for this series of books have made a lifelong impact on me.

—George Roy

With much love to my family, Robbie, Zachary, and Sarah, for your patience and support through this process. Your encouragement and love are beyond anything I could have asked for. Thank you to my parents, friends, and community for your endless support and encouragement in all things and my incredible colleagues, Juli, Ed, and George, for the determination and vision to see this book through.

—Janet Andreasen

Solution Tree Press would like to thank the following reviewers:

Cynthia Burke
Mathematics Teacher
Sherrard Middle School
Wheeling, West Virginia

Melissa Carli
Elementary Mathematics Program Specialist
Lake County Schools
Howey-in-the-Hills, Florida

Mary Jones
Mathematics Support and Advanced
  Mathematics
Southeast Bulloch Middle School
Brooklet, Georgia

Steve Leinwand
Principal Research Analyst
American Institutes for Research
Past President, National Council of Supervisors
  of Mathematics
Washington, DC

Becky Link
Mathematics Teacher
Fort Recovery Middle School
Fort Recovery, Ohio

Visit **go.solution-tree.com/mathematics** to download the free
reproducibles in this book.

Table of Contents

CHAPTER 5
Measurement and Geometry **105**

CHAPTER 6
Statistics and Probability. **133**

EPILOGUE
Next Steps 149

References 153

Index. 155

About the Authors

Edward C. Nolan is preK–12 director of mathematics for Montgomery County Public Schools in Maryland. He has nineteen years of classroom experience in both middle and high schools and was department chair for fifteen years, all in Montgomery County. An active member of the National Council of Teachers of Mathematics (NCTM), he is currently the president of the Maryland Council of Supervisors of Mathematics. Nolan is also a consultant for Solution Tree as one of the leaders of Dixon Nolan Adams Mathematics, providing support for teachers and administrators on the rigorous standards for mathematics.

Nolan has been published in the *Banneker Banner*, a publication of the Maryland Council of Teachers of Mathematics, and *Mathematics Teaching in the Middle School*, an NCTM publication, and he has conducted professional development at the state, regional, and national levels, including webinars for NCTM and TODOS: Mathematics for ALL. His research interests lie in helping students and teachers develop algebraic thinking and reasoning. In 2005, Nolan won the Presidential Award for Excellence in Mathematics and Science Teaching.

He is a graduate of the University of Maryland. He earned a master's degree in educational administration from Western Maryland College.

To learn more about Nolan's work, follow @ed_nolan on Twitter.

Juli K. Dixon, PhD, is a professor of mathematics education at the University of Central Florida (UCF) in Orlando. She coordinates the award-winning Lockheed Martin/UCF Academy for Mathematics and Science for the K–8 master of education program as well as the mathematics track of the doctoral program in education. Prior to joining the faculty at UCF, Dr. Dixon was a secondary mathematics educator at the University of Nevada, Las Vegas and a public school mathematics teacher in urban school settings at the elementary, middle, and secondary levels.

She is a prolific writer who has authored and coauthored books, textbooks, chapters, and articles. A sought-after speaker, Dr. Dixon has delivered keynotes and other presentations throughout the United States. She has served as chair of the National Council of Teachers of Mathematics Student Explorations in Mathematics Editorial Panel and as a board member for the Association of Mathematics Teacher Educators. At the state level, she has served on the board of directors for the Nevada Mathematics Council and is a past president of the Florida Association of Mathematics Teacher Educators.

Dr. Dixon received a bachelor's degree in mathematics and education from State University of New York at Potsdam, a master's degree in mathematics education from Syracuse University, and a doctorate in curriculum and instruction with an emphasis in mathematics education from the University of Florida. Dr. Dixon is a leader in Dixon Nolan Adams Mathematics.

To learn more about her work supporting children with special needs, visit www.astrokeofluck.net and follow @thestrokeofluck on Twitter.

George J. Roy, PhD, is an assistant professor of mathematics education at the University of South Carolina, where he teaches mathematics methods courses as part of the middle-level education program in the Department of Instruction and Teacher Education. His research includes examining the uses of technology in middle school mathematics classrooms and preservice teachers' development of mathematical content knowledge. Dr. Roy was an elementary and middle-level mathematics educator at the University of South Florida St. Petersburg. He also served as a mathematics teacher in an urban middle school, where he earned a National Board for Professional Teaching Standards certification in mathematics/early adolescence.

Dr. Roy has authored and coauthored numerous articles and several book chapters and has presented at the annual conferences of the National Council of Teachers of Mathematics, Association of Mathematics Teacher Educators, and North American Chapter of the International Group for the Psychology of Mathematics Education.

He earned a bachelor's degree in mathematics from Rollins College, a master's degree in mathematics education (with a focus on K–8 mathematics and science) from the Lockheed Martin Academy at the University of Central Florida, and a doctorate in education (with an emphasis on mathematics education) from the University of Central Florida.

To learn more about Dr. Roy's work, follow @georgejroy on Twitter.

Janet B. Andreasen, PhD, is an associate lecturer of mathematics education at the University of Central Florida (UCF). She is the coordinator of secondary education and works with prospective and practicing mathematics teachers at the elementary, middle, and high school levels. Dr. Andreasen's research interests include examining mathematical knowledge for teaching and using technology to foster student learning of mathematical concepts. Prior to joining the faculty at UCF, Dr. Andreasen was a high school mathematics teacher.

Dr. Andreasen has published books, book chapters, and articles in state and national publications as well as provided professional presentations throughout the United States including for the National Council of Teachers of Mathematics, the Association of Mathematics Teacher Educators, and the Florida Council of Teachers of Mathematics. She is a member of the Association of Mathematics Teacher Educators, the National Council of Teachers of Mathematics, and the Florida Council of Teachers of Mathematics.

Dr. Andreasen received a bachelor's degree in biomedical engineering from the University of Miami and both a master's degree in mathematics education and a PhD in education and mathematics education from the University of Central Florida. Her dissertation focused on how prospective elementary school teachers come to understand whole number concepts and operations in meaningful ways for teaching through the use of classroom norms and explanations and justifications in a mathematics course for teachers.

To learn more about Dr. Andreasen's work, follow @JanetAndreasen on Twitter.

To book Edward C. Nolan, Juli K. Dixon, George J. Roy, or Janet B. Andreasen for professional development, contact pd@solution-tree.com.

Introduction

The only way to learn mathematics is to do mathematics.

—Paul Halmos

When teaching, much of the day is spent supporting students to engage in learning new content. In mathematics, that often means planning for instruction, delivering the planned lessons, and engaging in the formative assessment process. There are opportunities to attend conferences and other professional development events, but those are typically focused on teaching strategies or on administrative tasks like learning the new gradebook program. Opportunities to take on the role of *learner* of the subject you teach are often neglected. As you read *Making Sense of Mathematics for Teaching Grades 6–8*, you will have the chance to become the learner once again. You will *learn* about the mathematics you teach by *doing* the mathematics you teach.

There is a strong call to build teachers' content knowledge for teaching mathematics. A lack of a "deep understanding of the content that [teachers] are expected to teach may inhibit their ability to teach meaningful, effective, and connected lesson sequences, regardless of the materials that they have available" (National Council of Teachers of Mathematics [NCTM], 2014, p. 71). This lack of deep understanding may have more to do with lack of exposure than anything else.

All too often, exposure to mathematics is limited to rules that have little meaning. Teachers then pass these rules on to students. For example, how mathematics is taught in the middle grades influences students' understanding of mathematics in later years. A teacher might say "you cannot take the square root of a negative number" as a way to help reinforce student understanding that square numbers and their square roots are connected and that multiplying a number by itself will always result in a positive number. However, this becomes a problem when students are introduced to the imaginary number, *i*, in their study of quadratic functions. Using the square root of –1 is an important element in examining many different functional relationships in high school mathematics and beyond, and teachers need to be sure to present information in a way that does not create inappropriate meanings for future study. This is an example of what Karen Karp, Sarah Bush, and Barbara Dougherty (2014) refer to as *rules that expire*. Providing rules that work in the short term that cannot be applied in the long term is counterproductive to supporting students with meaningful school mathematics experiences. Teachers must attend to precision when teaching concepts in mathematics, or students will learn incorrect information. Students will need to later unlearn those misconceptions—and unlearning a concept is much more difficult than learning it correctly the first time. This happens when teachers are not afforded the opportunity to develop a deep understanding of the mathematics they teach.

This book is our response to requests from teachers, coaches, supervisors, and administrators who understand the need to know mathematics for teaching but who don't know how to reach a deeper level of content knowledge or to support others to do so. First and foremost, the book provides guidance for refining what it means to be a teacher of mathematics. To teach mathematics for depth means to facilitate instruction that empowers students to develop a deep understanding of mathematics. This can happen when teachers are equipped with strong mathematics content knowledge—knowledge that covers the conceptual understanding and procedural skill of mathematics and knowledge that is supported by a variety of strategies and tools for engaging students to learn mathematics. With these elements as a backdrop, this book can be used to go below the surface in core areas of mathematics.

Second, coaches, supervisors, and administrators benefit from the content and perspectives provided in this book because it offers a source that supports guidance and mentoring to enhance teachers' mathematics content knowledge and their knowledge for teaching mathematics. They can particularly benefit from this book as a resource for helping them recognize expected norms in mathematics classrooms.

Here, we will set the stage for what you will learn from this book along with the rationale for why it is important for you to learn it. First, we provide some of the reasons why teachers need to understand mathematics with depth. Next, we share the structure of each chapter along with a description of what you will experience through that structure. Finally, we present ways that you will be able to use this book as an individual or within a collaborative team.

A Call for Making Sense of Mathematics for Teaching

Often, teachers are not initially aware that they lack sufficient depth of mathematical understanding or that this depth of understanding is critical to being equipped to guide students' mathematical development. What we have found is that engaging in tasks designed to contrast conceptual and procedural solution processes provides a window into the gap left by teaching mathematics without understanding.

Procedural skill includes the ability to follow rules for operations with a focus on achieving a solution quickly, while *conceptual understanding* includes comprehension of mathematical ideas, operations, and relationships. The procedure for dividing fractions is one that most teachers can execute without much thought, yet the conceptual understanding needed to compose a word problem that requires dividing fractions to solve and to draw a picture to solve the same problem might be less accessible. Thus, the contrast between typical solution processes and those that develop conceptual understanding highlights the need to truly know mathematics in order to teach it.

As a team, we provide large-scale professional development workshops for school districts across the United States and beyond. We often begin our presentations by engaging participants in a short mathematical activity to set the stage for the types of mind-shifting approaches necessary to teach for depth. One such activity involves considering different ways to compare ratios within a real-world context. Consider the comparison in the task in figure I.1.

> Arianna is making an orange drink for her birthday party. She has decided to try two different mixtures. For the first one, Arianna mixes 3 quarts of orange juice with 4 quarts of ginger ale. For the second one, she mixes 5 quarts of orange juice with 6 quarts of ginger ale. Which drink will have the stronger orange taste? How do you know?

Figure I.1: Ratio reasoning task.

Participants frequently use one of two strategies to solve this problem. Some participants show that the part-to-part relationship of the first drink is 0.75 (by dividing 3 by 4). Next, they determine that the part-to-part relationship of the second drink is 0.8$\overline{3}$ (by dividing 5 by 6). With these values, they determine that the second drink has the stronger orange taste, as 0.8$\overline{3}$ is greater than 0.75.

Other participants often compare the two ratios and represent them using fraction notation as ¾ [?] ⅚. They also use language commonly used with fractions to describe them, such as *numerators* and *denominators*. Next, they use a form of a cross-products strategy, multiplying 4 × 5 and 6 × 3 to determine that the product of one "diagonal" is 18 and the product of the other "diagonal" is 20. Using this information, they determine that ¾ is less than ⅚ because 18 is less than 20 (see figure I.2).

Therefore, the first drink is weaker than the second one because ¾ is less than ⅚ (actually, because 18 is less than 20).

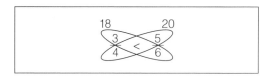

Figure I.2: Solving an open proportion.

While both of these processes provide the correct answer to the relationship, the challenge comes when the participants are asked to justify their solution process and provide support for the procedure they used. In the first solution, while they understand how the fractions are equivalent to the decimal representations, they are not sure what the 0.75 and the 0.8$\overline{3}$ represent in the context of the problem. In thinking of this as a part-to-part relationship and representing the quantities as decimals, the connection to the strength of the orange taste is lost. The decimal representations are the rate of the quantity of orange juice for each unit of ginger ale, but this is a difficult connection to see and to associate with the original context of taste of the overall drink, which is a part-to-whole relationship.

In the second solution pathway, participants struggle to determine the meaning of 18 and 20 in the context of the problem. This process is actually a way to think of the amount of orange juice in terms of the same amount of ginger ale for each mixture. The 18 refers to 18 quarts of orange juice to 24 quarts of ginger ale and the 20 refers to 20 quarts of orange juice to 24 quarts of ginger ale. However, the 24 quarts of ginger ale, is implied with this method. Since both amounts of orange juice are mixed with the same amount of ginger ale, the conclusion that 20 quarts of orange juice would make the drink have a stronger orange taste compared to 18 quarts of orange juice makes sense. Again, without this extended explanation, the connection to the context of the original problem is lost. This method, sometimes referred to as the "butterfly method," is an example of a process that you can use to get a correct answer without understanding why the process works or what it means in the context of the problem.

How can the context support reasoning about the task? For the first drink, Arianna is combining 3 quarts of orange juice with 4 quarts of ginger ale, so she ends up with 7 quarts of the drink mixture. The question asked relates to which drink will have the stronger orange taste, so the relative amount of orange juice to the amount of the drink can be described with the ratio ³⁄₇, or 3 quarts of orange juice to 7 quarts of drink. For the second drink, she mixes 5 quarts of orange juice to 6 quarts of ginger ale, or a ratio of ⁵⁄₁₁, relating orange juice to the total number of quarts in the second drink. This allows you to compare the part-to-whole relations for the two different drink examples. This provides a closer tie to the context of the problem. How do you compare the ratios of ³⁄₇ and ⁵⁄₁₁? You might consider using a benchmark value, such as ½; however, *both* ratios are slightly less than ½. Because of this, using the benchmark of ½ will take a bit more effort. The orange juice part of each mixture is half a part away from being half of the mixture. The comparison would involve making sense of that half of a part. Since each of the 11 parts of the second mixture are smaller than each of the seven parts of the first mixture, the $5/11$ is closer to ½ than $3/7$ because it is half of a smaller part away from making up one-half of the mixture. This is correct reasoning, and mathematically justified, but it can be confusing to understand.

Another way to solve this problem is to create a whole that has an equal number of total quarts in both mixtures and then compare the number of parts that are orange juice in each mixture. If you made 11 batches of the first drink compared to 7 batches of the second drink, both would have 77 quarts in total. The ratios, $33/77$ and $35/77$, then lead to the conclusion that the second drink will have the stronger orange taste. Both of these methods obtain the same correct answer as the earlier ones, but these methods involve making sense of the problem and connecting the solution process to the context of the problem.

Teachers who do not have this depth of understanding may miss opportunities to develop it in their students. They must also understand how content is developed from one year to the next, use effective mathematics practices to build mathematical proficiency in all students, and incorporate tasks, questioning, and evidence into instruction.

Understanding Mathematics for Teaching

How does one develop proportional reasoning? Development of proportional reasoning happens best when there is an opportunity to apply ratio and proportion concepts and skills in a variety of contexts. Even if *you* have this understanding, how do you help your fellow teachers or the teachers you support develop the same? Questions such as these led us to create our mathematics-content-focused professional development institutes and the accompanying follow-up workshops, in which teachers implement new skills and strategies learned at the mathematics institutes. Conversations during the follow-up workshops provide evidence that teachers benefit from knowing the mathematics with depth, as do the students they serve. After all, discussing how to make sense of ratios within teacher teams is a powerful way to develop a deep understanding.

We begin each follow-up workshop with a discussion of what is going well at the participants' schools and what needs further attention. Their responses to both queries reaffirm our need to focus on teachers' pedagogical content knowledge. A typical response regarding what is going well includes a discussion about how teachers are now able to make mathematical connections between the topics they teach. Teachers begin to recognize commonalities between topics, such as the connection between similarity and proportional reasoning; they might explore the relationship between a scale drawing and a real object and reflect back to their earlier discussions with students about ratios and proportions. They reconnect the idea of unit rate and multiplicative reasoning when they discuss finding the relationship between the scale drawing and the actual object. Teachers report that, in past years, they taught these two content areas as separate topics, making no connections to the importance of flexible understanding across mathematics, as though the topics existed in silos, completely separate. They taught without coherence. With a deeper understanding of their content, however, they note that they are able to reinforce earlier topics and provide rich experiences as they make connections from one topic to the next. Similarly, coaches report that their deeper mathematics understanding is useful in helping teachers attend to these connections during planning and instruction and within the formative assessment process. The formative assessment process includes the challenging work of evaluating student understanding throughout the mathematics lesson and unit. Teachers need a deep understanding of the mathematics they teach to support a thoughtful process of making sense of student thinking and being confident to respond to students' needs whether those needs include filling gaps, addressing common errors, or advancing ideas beyond the scope of the lesson or unit.

Through the mathematics institutes and workshops, participants realize the need for additional professional development experiences, but providing this level of support can be challenging for schools and districts. This book is our response to this need. We've designed it to support stakeholders who want a review as well as to address additional topics. Our approach herein is informed by our extensive experience providing professional development throughout the United States as well as internationally and is supported by research on best practices for teaching and learning mathematics.

Engaging in the Mathematical Practices

As teachers of mathematics, our goal for all students should be mathematical proficiency, regardless of the standards used. One way to achieve mathematical proficiency is to "balance *how* to use mathematics with *why* the mathematics works" (National Council of Supervisors of Mathematics [NCSM], 2014, pp. 20–21, emphasis added). Mathematical proficiency involves unpacking the mathematics embedded within learning progressions, developing and implementing an assortment of strategies connected to mathematical topics and the real world, being able to explain and justify mathematical procedures, and interpreting and making sense of students' thinking (Ball, Thames, & Phelps, 2008). These processes are well described by the eight Standards for Mathematical Practice contained within the Common Core State Standards (CCSS) for mathematics (National Governors Association Center for Best Practices [NGA] & Council of Chief State School Officers [CCSSO], 2010).

1. Make sense of problems and persevere in solving them.

2. Reason abstractly and quantitatively.

3. Construct viable arguments and critique the reasoning of others.

4. Model with mathematics.

5. Use appropriate tools strategically.

6. Attend to precision.

7. Look for and make use of structure.

8. Look for and express regularity in repeated reasoning.

The Mathematical Practices describe the ways that mathematically proficient students solve problems and engage in learning mathematics. What does this mean to you and your students? Since the Mathematical Practices truly describe how *students* engage with the mathematics, your role becomes that of facilitator, supporting this engagement. Think about asking your students to solve the equation $3(x - 7) = 42$. If your goal of instruction is for students to think about the different pathways to solve for x, in what ways should the students engage in this task? If you want them to consider that they could either divide both sides of the equation by 3 first, or they could distribute the 3 on the left side of the equation first, then you want them to be open to thinking about the structure of the equation and not focus on a step-by-step procedure for equation solving. Students who look at the structure of an equation and reason that since both sides of the equation are multiples of 3, dividing by 3 may be an efficient method, are making sense of the process of solving equations in flexible ways. That is, they are making sense of both the application of properties of operations *and* using their number sense as they look for "friendly" numbers. This is something that might be missed without an emphasis on Mathematical Practice 7, "Look for and make use of structure." How should teachers facilitate this sort of discussion with students so that the teachers are not doing all the telling (and thinking)? It requires instruction that acknowledges the value of students talking about mathematics and using mathematics to communicate their ideas.

When the mathematics content and the mathematical practices are addressed in tandem, students have the best opportunity to develop clarity about mathematics reasoning and what it means to do mathematics successfully.

Emphasizing the TQE Process

As part of the professional development material in this book, we include videos of grades 6–8 classroom episodes (and occasionally grades leading to and extending from this grade band) in which students explore rich mathematical tasks. Classroom videos from grades before and after grades 6–8 provide the opportunity to highlight the importance of prerequisite concepts and skills as well as links to the mathematics on the horizon. For example, one of the included videos shows high school students interpreting a real-world graph in order to demonstrate how similar strategies that students develop in the middle grades connect to interpreting representations later in their mathematics career. In presenting these videos, we emphasize three key aspects of the teacher's role—(1) tasks, (2) questioning, and (3) evidence—which make up what we call the *TQE process*.

Our emphasis on the TQE process helps define a classroom that develops mathematics as a focused, coherent, and rigorous subject. Thus, we uphold the following tenets.

- **Teachers with a deep understanding of the content they teach select *tasks* that provide students with the opportunity to engage in practices that support learning concepts before procedures; they know that for deep learning to take place, students need to understand the procedures they use.** Students who engage in mathematical tasks are also engaged in learning mathematics with understanding. Consider grade 8 students who are making sense of strategies to interpret systems of linear equations. The sequence of considering the correct number of solutions is important to address a specific learning goal. For example, if the goal is for students to make sense of the intersection of distinct lines, students would be presented with examples of lines with a variety of combinations of slopes in order to consider the type of intersection that would be represented. From examples of intersecting lines, students would be directed to explore patterns in pairs of equations with the same slope. Once students identify the pattern, they can be led to see why lines with the same slope and the same y-intercept have an infinite number of solutions and lines with the same slope and different y-intercepts have no solutions. Consider finding the number of solutions to the system $y = 4x - 12$ and $y = 4x - 8$. Students should know that the graphs of both of these equations would have the rate of change of 4 and that they have different y-intercepts without having to actually graph them.

Students should reason that since the graphed lines would have the same rate of change and different *y*-intercepts, they would not intersect, and therefore the equations have no solutions in common. These students are making sense of patterns in the characteristics of lines as a way of determining the solutions of linear systems. Thus, this scenario provides insight into a classroom where carefully selected tasks support deeper learning.

- **Teachers who have a deep understanding of the content they teach facilitate targeted and productive *questioning* strategies because they have a clear sense of how the content progresses within and across grades.** For instance, in the grade 8 example, teachers would facilitate discussions around strategies for finding solutions to systems of linear equations that focus on making meaning from the characteristics of lines and how those properties are important in determining the number of solutions to a system. Teachers ask questions such as "What do you know about lines that have the same rate of change?" to draw students' attention to how the characteristics of lines can help determine the number of solutions to a linear system without having to graph the lines.

- **Teachers who have a deep understanding of the content they teach use *evidence* gained from the formative assessment process to help them know where to linger in developing students' coherent understanding of mathematics.** In the grade 8 example, teachers know it is important for students to explore multiple representations and characteristics of lines to make sense of systems and that these tools are more important than a process that focuses on rules and procedures. They look for evidence that students are using strategies based on using appropriate representations and reasoning about the properties of lines to make sense of systems of linear equations rather than using procedures that might not be efficient, or worse, might be poorly understood.

Throughout the book and the accompanying classroom videos, we share elements of the TQE process to help you as both a learner and a teacher of mathematics. In addition, we ask that you try to answer three targeted questions as you watch each video. These questions are as follows:

1. How does the teacher prompt the students to make sense of the problem?

2. How do the students engage in the task; what tools or strategies are the students using to model the task?

3. How does the teacher use questioning to engage students in thinking about their thought processes?

Next, we describe the structure of the book to help guide your reading.

The Structure of Making Sense

To address the mathematical content taught in the middle grades, each chapter focuses on a different overarching topic. For instance, chapter 1 examines fraction operations and integer concepts and operations. Chapter 2 then explores ratios and proportional relationships. Chapter 3 takes a look at equations, expressions, and inequalities, and chapter 4 addresses functions. Chapter 5 examines measurement and geometry, and chapter 6 closes with a focus on statistics and probability. These topics represent the big ideas for the middle grades. Each chapter concludes with a series of questions to prompt reflection on the topic under discussion.

We end the book with an epilogue featuring next steps to help you and your team make sense of mathematics for teaching and implement this important work in your school or district.

To further break down each overarching topic, each chapter shares a common structure: The Challenge, The Progression, The Mathematics, The Classroom, and The Response.

The Challenge

Each chapter begins with an opportunity for you to engage in an initial task connected to the chapter's big idea. We call this section The Challenge because this task might challenge your thinking. We encourage you to stop and engage with the task before reading further—to actually *do* the task. Throughout the book, we alert you to the need to stop and do tasks with a *do now* symbol (see figure I.3).

Figure I.3: *Do now* symbol.

The presentation of mathematical ideas in this book may be different from how you learned mathematics. Consider being asked to estimate the quotient of $5\frac{2}{3} \div \frac{5}{6}$. This task may test your understanding of the mathematical topic being explored. You might eventually be asked to draw a picture of the process you could use to find the quotient, something you may or may not have tried in your own mathematics learning. Tasks in these sections focus on reasoning and sense making, since the rules of mathematics are developed through connections to earlier mathematical experiences rather than through procedures presented without meaning.

Since one purpose of this book is to engage you as a learner *and* teacher of mathematics, the tasks we ask you to explore support this goal. As a student of mathematics, you will consider how you learn mathematics. As a teacher of mathematics, you will explore how this newly found understanding could be the impetus for making sense of mathematics for teaching.

The Progression

Mathematics content knowledge is not enough. According to NCSM (2014), teachers must also "*understand how to best sequence, connect, and situate the content they are expected to teach within learning progressions*" (p. 24, emphasis in original). This means teachers need to know both the mathematics for their grade level and the mathematics that comes before and after their grade level—how the mathematics progresses over time.

Thus, each chapter highlights a progression of learning for a big idea. These progressions identify how learning develops over multiple years and highlight the importance of making sense of each building block along the way. The sequences defined by the progressions help the learner—and the teacher—make sense of the big idea in question. Understanding how content progresses provides avenues for supporting both the learner who struggles and the learner who needs enrichment.

Our placement of topics within grades was informed by the Common Core State Standards for mathematics (NGA & CCSSO, 2010). However, discussion of how the mathematics is developed within the progressions was not limited by this interpretation. We do not refer to specific content standards from the Common Core in an effort to expand the discussion to include *all* rigorous mathematics standards including those found outside of the United States. Note that because learning progressions develop over time, there will be occasions when this book addresses topics that reach into the intermediate grades or high school.

The Mathematics

There is much talk about rigor in instruction these days, but what does *rigor* mean in the context of teaching and learning mathematics? A misnomer is that rigor means *hard* or *difficult*. Rather, *rigor* refers to the need to incorporate all forms of thinking about mathematics—including concepts, procedures, the language of mathematics, and applications—in the teaching and learning process. However, this raises several questions. What does this actually look like in instruction? What teacher actions expose all students to rigor? How do you balance rigor reflected by reasoning and sense making with the ability to memorize an area formula?

Consider the formula for the area of a trapezoid, $A_{trap} = \frac{1}{2}(b_1 + b_2)h$. You know this formula; you probably know it without needing to think. Yet what path do teachers use to bring students to this level? All too often it begins and ends with memorization. Some students are able to memorize the formula. Some are not. Is this an example of teaching with rigor? The answer is no.

Importantly, rigor includes making sense of formulas by justifying connections to other known formulas. Sense making and conceptual development should precede a focus on memorization, rules, and procedures. This is where teaching might get uncomfortable. You may not have been taught the strategies as a student or see the connections. Thus, within The Mathematics section in each chapter, you will unpack the big ideas so the mathematics is explicitly connected to ways of making this knowledge accessible and rigorous for your students. For example, think about how the area formulas for known shapes, such as rectangles and triangles, can be used to build a formula to determine the area of a trapezoid. Exploring mathematics in this way develops a deep personal understanding of mathematics. As you develop this understanding, procedures and algorithms will make sense, and you will be able to explain and justify them (NCTM, 2014). Through this process, we will support you in developing the knowledge to promote students' procedural fluency, which is defined as "skill in carrying out procedures flexibly, accurately, efficiently, and appropriately" (Kilpatrick, Swafford, & Findell, 2001, p. 116).

Many of the tasks throughout this book can be characterized as high-cognitive-demand tasks, which are "tasks that require students to think conceptually and that stimulate students to make connections that lead to a different set of opportunities for student thinking" (Stein & Smith, 1998, p. 269). Consideration for the understanding, creation, selection, and implementation of high-cognitive-demand tasks is vital for effective mathematics learning (Dixon, Adams, & Nolan, 2015). While including tasks that are high and low cognitive demand supports a balance of conceptual understanding and procedural fluency, the cognitive demand of tasks often declines during instruction when the cognitive complexity of the task is not maintained (Kisa & Stein, 2015). How will you maintain the challenge of tasks through your actions? In this section and throughout the book, we provide you with excerpts from mathematics lessons so you can build a shared understanding of what mathematics instruction can look like in classrooms. In addition, we emphasize one or more of the best-aligned Mathematical Practices that support the learning of the relevant mathematics content. This is important regardless of whether you are teaching using the Common Core State Standards for mathematics. It describes effective teaching and learning of any mathematical content.

The Classroom

In what ways do you support student learning in the mathematics classroom? For instance, do you encourage student discourse? Doing so allows you to consider what students are talking about and how you will respond to their talk. Your approach to student talk—and many other classroom aspects—helps determine the type of classroom learning community you and your students develop together. This classroom learning community is critical to the development of students' deep mathematical understanding.

The Classroom sections provide videos and extensive descriptions of what happens in engaging mathematics lessons. In order to assist you in thinking about how classrooms that develop mathematical understanding should look, each chapter includes two video episodes. These short videos show students exploring one task from the big idea of that chapter and one task from a related big idea. When you see the play button, please stop and watch the video. Included with the icon is the accompanying web address and a Quick Response (QR) code for you to access the video.

          www.solution-tree.com/Dividing_Fractions_in_Context

We consider the accompanying videos to be a further investment in our effort to support the teaching and learning of mathematics. You will have the opportunity to see the topics we write about in the book in action. For instance, when we discuss how to massage a task so that it engages students, elicits student talk, and uncovers students' errors, we then follow up by capturing the essence of these actions in real classrooms. This modeling of good mathematics teaching provides opportunities for teachers to discuss what is happening in their own classrooms with the same mathematics content. It is not always possible for teachers to leave the classroom to observe a fellow teacher engaged in mathematics instruction. Thus, these videos help fill this gap and also provide a context for teachers to try an approach to mathematics teaching as modeled in the videos.

You must also consider the classroom expectations set for students. For instance, what are the rules for students answering questions? These rules should be established and made explicit for students so they know what you expect of them when they work on tasks. Also, how do students work together on tasks? Students can benefit greatly from collaborative experiences in mathematics, but they need to know how to best collaborate with each other. In many instances, the student who is confident and right most of the time does most of the talking. Thus, helping students monitor and regulate their discourse is valuable for the mathematics learning experience. As illustrated in the classroom videos, we encourage three classroom norms for every mathematics classroom.

1. Explain and justify solutions.

2. Make sense of each other's solutions.

3. Say when you don't understand or when you don't agree.

The classroom norms need to support the active thinking of students rather than solely relying on the thinking of teachers, as is so often the case in teacher-centered classrooms. This point is true when students work on their own as well as when students work together. You should always provide students the opportunity to share their strategies and make sense of the thinking of other students in order to be sure they understand mathematics with depth.

The structure of the classroom needs to support the thinking and learning of the students, and different tasks may require different structures. Some tasks may include questions that help students make connections; other tasks may not need such support. One model that is often discussed in many schools and districts is the gradual release of responsibility, commonly described as the teaching practice where the teacher models ("I do"), then the class practices together ("We do"), and finally the students practice independently ("You do") (Fisher & Frey, 2003). Although this method is appropriate at times, we advocate for methods that include focus on the *students* making sense of and reasoning with mathematics. An alternative approach for mathematics is what we call *layers of facilitation*.

1. *I facilitate the whole class* to engage in meaningful tasks through questioning.

2. *I facilitate small groups* to extend the learning initiated in the whole-group setting.

3. *I facilitate individuals* to provide evidence of their understanding of the learning goal.

This change in teacher role focuses on the teacher as a facilitator of knowledge acquisition rather than as a transmitter of knowledge. As you read the text and as you watch the videos, you will notice our focus is largely on implementing layers of facilitation, but it is important to recognize that there are some topics and mathematical content that need to be taught following the gradual release of responsibility model. It is important for you, as the teacher, to determine when to apply this model. Keep in mind that students will benefit from opportunities to have a more participatory role during instruction whenever possible.

The Response

How do you respond when students struggle? What do you do when students express misconceptions? It is important to use student errors as springboards for learning; the errors and the gaps in prerequisite knowledge that lead to those errors inform your everyday instruction as well as your response to intervention (RTI) process within a Multi-Tiered System of Supports (MTSS).

Again, consider how students approach finding the area of a trapezoid. Perhaps they use their recall of the formula, or maybe they use other strategies to determine the area. Think about questions you could ask in order to gather information about students' thinking processes, both when they have the correct answer and when they do not. If your students do not multiply by ½ when finding the area of a trapezoid, how can you help them examine their thinking and correct their mistake without simply giving them the correct answer? One approach would be to ask questions to support the efforts of your students and encourage them to think of errors as beneficial in order to learn mathematics with depth. This is an area where your own depth of mathematical understanding is critical to help your students develop their thinking.

It is essential to explore your students' reasoning and sense making and break down that thinking in order to rebuild their understanding of mathematics. Effective teachers understand what models and strategies best support students in ways that allow them to connect their current thinking with the learning goal of the task. You can then use the evidence of the level of students' understanding you gather to inform your response both during and after instruction.

Now that you understand what is to come in the following pages, here's how we suggest you approach the book.

How to Use This Book

Collaborative teams of teachers can use this book to explore mathematics content and engage in discussions about teacher actions that will help bring mathematics to life for students. In fact, the entire TQE process is best accomplished by a collaborative team working together to address the four critical questions—the guiding force of the professional learning community (PLC) culture (DuFour, DuFour, Eaker, & Many, 2010):

1. What do we want students to learn and be able to do?

2. How will we know if they know it?

3. How will we respond if they don't know it?

4. How will we respond if they do know it?

This book is an optimal tool for your collaborative team in a PLC culture. Although it is grade-band specific, it also provides support for vertical (across grades) discussions and planning. There are many topics in this book that can be addressed in your grade-level team or in your vertical team, including the Mathematical Practices. While the Mathematical Practices are not grade specific, how students engage with them can be expected to vary from grade to grade, and you can benefit from grade-specific as well as vertical discussions about them.

Our expectation is that individuals or collaborative teams will be able to use this book by reading the chapters in order. Within each chapter, we help you develop clarity about the mathematical content and its progression. Teachers often have questions about the sequence of mathematics content in mathematics texts and other resources—sometimes the sequence is aligned with authentic progressions and sometimes not. Thus, you can use this book as a resource to understand how background and underlying knowledge of mathematics support further understanding and how to best align mathematics curriculum with the progression of the content.

We hope this book and the accompanying videos will be your go-to source for a deep dive into relevant mathematics content, effective pedagogical actions, appropriate classroom norms, meaningful assessment, and collaborative teacher team efforts. Our goal is for this resource to connect the good work of mathematics teaching that you are already facilitating with the goals of improving mathematics teaching that you aspire to attain.

CHAPTER 1

Fraction Operations and Integer Concepts and Operations

This chapter connects fraction-based content from the elementary grades to fraction operations in the middle grades. We begin with explorations that are grounded in elementary-level topics to help you support learners who have likely learned fractions in ways unlike how you may have developed your own understanding. These experiences are connected to topics in the middle grades to help you link these explorations to middle-grades content. This chapter also links early work with whole numbers to solving problems involving integers.

Fraction and integer operation sense is developed by embedding these operations in context through word problems. The word problems become valuable sense-making tools when visual models are used to solve them. Those visual solutions are then connected to equations, and finally, this process is connected to procedures by making sense of steps for solving the equations more efficiently. Results of following the procedures are checked through estimation to be sure solutions are reasonable.

The Challenge

The initial task in this chapter (see figure 1.1, page 16) begins this process by providing word problems to be solved with visual models. The three problems in figure 1.1 may be challenging if you have not previously explored representing fraction operations with drawings. The key is to create an image of the context of each problem with pictures—to act it out with your drawing. The discussion that follows will be much more meaningful if you make an attempt to solve each problem using a picture and then write the situation equation before proceeding with reading the chapter. A *situation equation* directly models the context of the problem but might not be used to solve the problem. This is contrasted with a *solution equation*, which can be used to solve a problem but might not actually model the problem as written. It is our position that the use of situation and solution equations provides a link between the word problem structure, the equations used to model the problem, and the solution process. Considering these different types of equations supports the connection between the structure of the word problem and the process of determining a solution, helping make sense of the mathematics, the operations, and the context of the problem.

Use a visual model to solve each problem so that the drawing represents the context of the problem. Do not simplify your answer. Then write an equation to model the situation.

1. There is ⅔ of a pie left over. Jessica ate ¾ of the leftover pie. How much of a whole pie did Jessica eat?

2. Tisa brought ¾ of a pan of brownies to school. Her friends ate ⅔ of what she brought. How much of a pan of brownies did her friends eat?

3. The park measured ⅔ of a mile by ¾ of a mile. What fraction of a square mile is the park?

Figure 1.1: Fraction multiplication in context task.

How did you begin to solve the first problem? What shape did you use to represent the pie? How did you identify the part of the pie that was left over? It is likely that you drew a circle to represent the region defined by the pie, partitioned into three equal parts, and shaded two of them to indicate the pie that was left over as illustrated in figure 1.2.

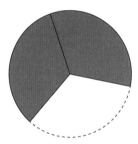

Figure 1.2: Two-thirds of a pie left over.

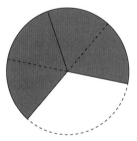

Figure 1.3: Partitioning the two third-size pieces to make four equal pieces.

If you drew a rectangle to represent the pie, you are not representing the context of the problem with your drawing (unless you have an unusual pie dish!). Research indicates that students are more likely to use visual models like drawings or physical models like manipulatives that match the context of the problem when they are first making sense of an operation with fractions (Dixon, Andreasen, Roy, Wheeldon, & Tobias, 2011). Teachers should support this process with models that correspond to the context of the problem.

You have your circle with ⅔ of the circle shaded. Now you need to determine how much Jessica ate. She ate ¾ of what is represented by the shaded region. The two shaded pieces need to be partitioned so that ¾ of the two pieces can be determined. The most direct route is to cut each of those two pieces into two equal pieces, making four shaded pieces as illustrated in figure 1.3. If you partitioned each third into four equal pieces, you might be forcing the picture to follow a procedure that mirrors the algorithm by creating twelve equal pieces in the whole like you do when you multiply the 3 and the 4 in the denominators of the factors in the problem.

Finding ¾ of the four shaded pieces is straightforward, but how do you name those three pieces? They need to be named in terms of the original pie. The part of the pie that was missing at the beginning of the problem—the third piece of the pie—needs to be thought of as two equal pieces as well. This is a place where errors are often made, and you need to remember the importance of connecting the concept of fraction—that all of the pieces in the whole have to be the same size—to this context. That means the entire pie needs to be described as equal parts—in this case, six equal pieces—and Jessica ate ³⁄₆ of the whole pie, as illustrated in figure 1.4. Since the directions indicated to not simplify the result, you should leave the product in this form rather than changing it to ½. These directions are important to follow when using visual models to solve fraction problems because if you simplify the fraction, it is no longer directly representative of your picture and it can mask the thinking and reasoning that you used to solve the problem.

The drawing in figure 1.4 clearly represents the context of the problem. You began with ⅔ of a pie and partitioned the two third-sized pieces into two equal-sized pieces each so that there would be four equal-sized pieces. Then you shaded to indicate what ¾ of that leftover pie would be in terms of the original whole pie and found that Jessica ate ³⁄₆ of the original pie. How do you represent this in equation form? How do you model this mathematically?

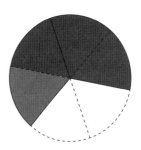

Figure 1.4: Three-sixths of the original pie is shaded.

Since you are finding a part of a part of a whole, you are multiplying. You know that ⅔ and ¾ need to be multiplied, but in what order? While the product is the same, the order in which you multiply matters when you want to preserve the context of the problem, such as with situation equations. When multiplication is originally presented to students using whole numbers, the first factor usually designates the number of groups and the second factor designates the number of objects in each group. With fractions, this structure can be modeled if the first factor represents part of a group and the second factor represents part of the whole. In essence, you are finding a part of a part of a whole. For the first problem in figure 1.1, are you multiplying ⅔ × ¾ or ¾ × ⅔?

Many teachers—and students—are quick to respond that the problem is represented by ⅔ × ¾ because ⅔ is the first factor mentioned in the word problem. However, if you think of finding groups of objects, you see that you are finding a part of a group of a part of a whole. Two-thirds represents the part of the whole, so you are finding ¾ of ⅔ of a pie or ¾ × ⅔. The equation to model this problem is ¾ × ⅔ = ³⁄₆. Some may model this situation as ¾ × ⅔ = ⁶⁄₁₂ instead, but this might be overemphasizing the standard algorithm of multiplying the numerators then the denominators. (This standard algorithm might be better named as the U.S. standard algorithm because there are other algorithms standard to other countries. In this book, standard algorithms will refer to the most common U.S. standard algorithms unless otherwise noted.) The product in an equation does not need to be the result of applying the algorithm. You found the product by showing your reasoning through a picture. If your picture resulted in ³⁄₆ of the pie being shaded, it is appropriate to record the situation equation as ¾ × ⅔ = ³⁄₆.

You may want to revisit the second problem in figure 1.1 before reading on. The discussion regarding the first problem might change your response to the second problem. When considering going back to examine your work, you are responding appropriately to the task. Experiences with the curriculum should alter how you think about future work. This is an example of moving along a learning trajectory and how carefully selected tasks and experiences with those tasks move learning forward.

In the second problem, Tisa brings ¾ of a pan of brownies to school. You probably shaded ¾ of a rectangle in a way similar to one of the two illustrations in figure 1.5 (page 18)—both represent the problem context. The first illustration will be used for the purpose of this discussion.

 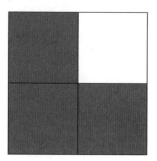

Figure 1.5: Three-fourths of a pan of brownies illustrated in two different ways.

At this point, it becomes obvious if you are simply drawing the algorithm by following a set of procedures for visually representing fraction multiplication or if you are acting out the problem using drawings. If you divided each of the fourths into three equal pieces to make twelve pieces in all, you might be following a procedure, thus losing some of the value in using visual representations to build fraction operation sense. Looking at the drawing in figure 1.5, you realize that there are three pieces shaded and Tisa's friends ate ⅔ of that shaded region, or two of the three shaded pieces. It is enough to identify those two shaded pieces in terms of the whole pan of brownies to solve this problem as illustrated in figure 1.6.

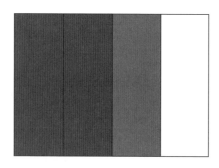

Figure 1.6: Illustration of ⅔ of ¾ of the pan of brownies.

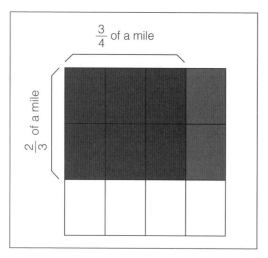

Figure 1.7: A park measuring ⅔ of a mile by ¾ of a mile.

With this problem, the result is represented by ²⁄₄ of a pan of brownies and the operation is multiplication, since you are finding parts of parts of objects. The equation would again include one of these two expressions: ⅔ × ¾ or ¾ × ⅔. This situation describes finding ⅔ of ¾ of a pan of brownies, so ⅔ × ¾ = ²⁄₄ is the situation equation.

The third problem describes the portion of a square mile covered by a park. The visual should represent a fraction of a square, with the square designating the square mile and the darker shaded region designating the park. An illustration supporting this solution process is provided in figure 1.7. First, ⅔ of the entire square mile was shaded, then ¾ of the shaded part was shaded.

Note that because this problem describes a portion of an area and the entire region is a square, either dimension can serve as the base or height. Therefore, the situation equation can be either ⅔ × ¾ = ⁶⁄₁₂ or ¾ × ⅔ = ⁶⁄₁₂. The illustration would be slightly different if ¾ of the entire square mile was shaded first and then ⅔ of that shaded portion was then shaded. The problem could also be solved by shading ⅔ of the entire square mile and then ¾ of the entire square mile using the area included in both shaded portions to determine the area of the park. Regardless of the slight differences in shading, the product for this situation is representative of the illustration as well as the result of performing the standard algorithm for multiplying fractions.

With which mathematical practices were you engaged as you explored this task? If the task was presented in a way that was unfamiliar to you, you were likely engaged in Mathematical Practice 1, "Make sense of problems and persevere in solving them." First, you needed to make sense of using visual models for solving fraction multiplication problems, and then you may have engaged in a productive struggle as you worked to solve them. However, you were also engaged in Mathematical Practice 4, "Model with mathematics"—this mathematical practice refers to "mathematizing" a situation. In each case, you began with a word problem and modeled it visually as well as with an equation. You *mathematized* the situation. You saw that how the problem was modeled depended on the context of the problem, even though the product was the same in each case. Because of this, how the problems were ordered in the task was important; the progression helped develop understanding.

The third problem in the task most closely represents the standard algorithm, further reinforcing the need to order tasks intentionally. If the goal of instruction is to move from conceptual understanding to procedural fluency, as is our position, then it would make sense to provide students with experiences visually representing solutions to problems like the first two in this task before introducing them to problems like the third one in this task. This supports the need to unpack a progression for developing fraction operation sense and fluency.

The Progression

The development of fraction operations shared in this book is influenced by the position that conceptual understanding must precede procedural fluency to build mathematical proficiency. Much of this progression occurs in the elementary grades, as the work there provides the foundation for context in the middle grades. Following is a progression for the development of fraction operation sense that includes that foundational work.

- Make sense of adding and subtracting fractions with like denominators.
- Make sense of multiplying fractions by whole numbers.
- Make sense of adding and subtracting fractions involving unlike denominators.
- Make sense of multiplying fractions and mixed numbers.
- Make sense of dividing whole numbers by unit fractions and unit fractions by nonzero whole numbers.
- Make sense of dividing fractions and mixed numbers.

Here is a progression that focuses on integer concepts and operations that resides exclusively in the middle grades.

- Use positive and negative numbers to describe quantities having opposite directions or opposite values, and represent them in real-world contexts.
- Represent integers on the number line and in the coordinate plane.
- Interpret inequalities with integers and connect them to a number line diagram.

- Model adding and subtracting integers on a number line diagram.
- Make sense of multiplying and dividing integers.

The placement of topics within grades provides a window into how this content develops over time. Exploration of fraction operations is introduced in grade 4. Emphasis on fraction operations spans grades 4 through 6, and coherence is maintained by connecting to earlier work with whole number operations in the elementary grades. Integers are introduced in grade 6, and students make sense of operations with integers in grade 7.

Grade 4

Students in grade 4 explore addition and subtraction of fractions with like denominators, with and without context. The key is that students solve these problems with visual models rather than beginning with the standard algorithm of adding the numerators and keeping the denominator.

It might seem surprising that fraction multiplication is explored prior to adding and subtracting fractions with unlike denominators. However, it does make sense when it is linked back to how multiplication of whole numbers develops (see chapter 2 of *Making Sense of Mathematics for Teaching Grades 3–5* [Dixon, Nolan, Adams, Tobias, & Barmoha, 2016] for an extensive discussion of whole number multiplication). Multiplication of whole numbers is developed as repeated addition in grade 2 and ultimately as multiplication in grade 3. Similarly, fraction multiplication is developed as repeated addition of fractions in grade 4. This is why multiplication is limited to multiplying fractions by whole numbers like $3 \times \frac{1}{5}$. The problem $3 \times \frac{1}{5}$ can be thought of as three groups of $\frac{1}{5}$ or $\frac{1}{5} + \frac{1}{5} + \frac{1}{5}$ and can be represented using a visual model. (This connection to whole numbers is also made when introducing operations with integers in grade 7.) Viewing multiplication in this way provides the link between adding fractions with like denominators and multiplication. This topic is developed further in grade 5.

Grade 5

In grade 5, work with addition and subtraction is extended to adding and subtracting fractions with unlike denominators. First, students solve problems with and without context using visual models and eventually using equations. As students represent fraction addition problems with visual models and record their results using equations, they see a pattern emerge. Once the fractions are described as equal parts of the same-size whole through the process of finding like denominators, students simply need to add the parts they have, which is described by the numerators, to find the sum. Through exploration, they see that this pattern applies to fraction subtraction as well. Ultimately, the goal is for students to add and subtract fractions with like and unlike denominators without the need for visual models but with an understanding of why the procedure they use works. Furthermore, they need to be able to determine if their answers are reasonable. Estimating sums and differences is an excellent way to determine the reasonableness of these solutions.

Students extend work with multiplication to multiplying fractions by fractions with and without context using visual models or equations to find the product. The task in figure 1.1 (page 16) provided opportunities for you to solve fraction multiplication word problems using visual models. You used a situation equation to represent the context, not to determine the solution. Using an equation to solve typically means applying an algorithm—in this case, the algorithm of multiplying numerators and multiplying denominators to find the product. Regardless of the solution process, it is important to use estimation to check whether the product is reasonable. For example, in the first word problem in figure 1.1 (page 16), an answer of 3⁄6, or 1⁄2, is reasonable because you were finding 3⁄4 × 2⁄3 so you were finding less than a whole group of 2⁄3 but more than half of a group of 2⁄3; therefore, a reasonable product would be between 1⁄3 and 2⁄3.

Finally, fifth-grade students are introduced to fraction division but only with two specific structures. Students divide:

1. Whole numbers by unit fractions (a unit fraction is a fraction with a numerator of one), such as 6 ÷ 1⁄3
2. Unit fractions by nonzero whole numbers (they cannot divide by zero because it is indeterminate), such as 1⁄4 ÷ 2

Students encounter these structures with and without context. The structure determines the problem type for word problems. This will be discussed later in the chapter. Students solve these problems using visual models or equations. Solving problems like these using equations provides an excellent opportunity to begin to make sense of the *invert and multiply* algorithm for dividing fractions. This algorithm is further developed in grade 6.

Grade 6

In grade 6, students extend the work they began in grade 5 to divide fractions by fractions with and without context using visual models or equations. Students recall their experiences from grade 5 to make sense of the invert and multiply algorithm. They might even explore the common denominator algorithm for dividing fractions. In any case, they use estimation and their understanding of division to check the reasonableness of their results.

Integers are first introduced in grade 6 in context and represented on the number line. Because of this, representations of the number line extend in both directions from zero. To deepen understanding of variables, $-p$ is developed as the *opposite* of p, to be sure that it is seen as more than a negative value. The number line is presented both horizontally and vertically.

Ordering numbers, a concept first introduced in kindergarten with whole numbers, is again a focus as students order numbers, including negative numbers, on the number line. For example, they make sense of comparing numbers like –3 and –5 by positioning them on a number line. Some students find this to be more accessible using a vertical number line rather than an exclusive use of a horizontal number line.

Integers describe distance and direction from zero. Finding the absolute value of a number is introduced in grade 6 when students find the distance of a number from zero, not the direction. For example, –6 describes a distance from zero as well as a direction—the negative direction. The absolute value of –6, or |–6|, describes a location that is six units from zero but does not include direction. This becomes important as students also describe distances on the coordinate plane. The coordinate plane is an extension of the number line and combines the horizontal number line and the vertical number line with the intersection occurring at the zero point of each number line.

Grade 7

The number line continues to be a tool as seventh-grade students use it to represent addition and subtraction of integers. Just as with students in the elementary grades, students in seventh grade apply properties of operations to add, subtract, multiply, and divide integers. Students solve problems involving operations with integers in context and create contexts for problems when none are provided.

Throughout the progressions for fraction operations and integer concepts and operations, emphasis is on reasoning and sense making. Much of what students encounter is presented in context, through word problems. When students use algorithms, they are able to explain why those algorithms work.

The Mathematics

How do students come to make sense of algorithms like invert and multiply or "a positive times a negative is a negative"? How do teachers? Students in grades 6–8 need to learn to make sense of fraction operations in word problems, use manipulatives to compute with fractions, connect visual solutions to algorithms, and make sense of integers. Here, you will unpack the mathematics of fractions and integers, providing the background necessary to teach these topics with depth.

Making Sense of Fraction Operations in Word Problems

Which should come first, computation or word problems? Our position is that instruction should lead with word problems. Initially, students make sense of the word problems by acting them out, using manipulatives, drawings, or mental images. After students solve problems in this manner, they can represent the process they followed with symbols and operations—much like you did with the problems in figure 1.1 (page 16). Eventually, students will be able to skip the step of acting out the problem and write the equation directly. At that point, students are well on their way to developing fraction operation sense. Consider the problems in figure 1.8. Solve them by acting them out with drawings to represent your thinking, and think about how you determined which operation to use, and how your understanding of each operation helps you make the correct choice. You might also find it valuable to work with members of your collaborative team and compare your solution strategies.

Use drawings to represent the following problems. Write an equation to model each problem situation.

1. Carmen had ½ of a yard of ribbon. How much more ribbon does she need so she will have ⅚ of a yard of ribbon altogether?

2. Julio bought ½ of a pound of sliced turkey. He made four sandwiches with the same amount of turkey on each sandwich. How much of a pound of turkey was on each sandwich?

3. Ming plans to make 3 batches of chocolate cookies. One batch calls for ¾ of a cup of cocoa. How much cocoa will she need to make the cookies?

4. Blake and Jordan each bought the same type of candy bar. Blake ate ¾ of his candy bar, and Jordan ate ⅝ of his. How much more of a candy bar did Blake eat than Jordan?

5. Amanda has 3½ yards of fabric. If she uses ⅔ of a yard of fabric for each project, how many projects can she make?

Figure 1.8: Fraction operation word problems.

In the first problem, Carmen starts with ½ of a yard of ribbon and ends with ⅚ of a yard of ribbon. The goal is to find out how much she needs to get in order to have ⅚ of a yard. The drawing in figure 1.9 shows the ½ of a yard of ribbon she has to start and her goal of ⅚ of a yard of ribbon.

The answer to this problem is described by what is needed to go from ½ of a yard to ⅚ of a yard. You know from your work with equivalent fractions that ½ of a yard of ribbon can be renamed as ³⁄₆ of a yard of ribbon. You can see from the drawing that since Carmen has ³⁄₆ of a yard of ribbon, she would need ²⁄₆ of a yard of ribbon more to reach her goal of ⅚ of a yard of ribbon (see figure 1.10). Although ²⁄₆ is equivalent to ⅓, it is not necessary to simplify the fraction at this point because the simplified form is not as clear in the picture.

The drawing is fairly straightforward, as is determining the answer. However, what situation equation would you use to represent the action in this problem? While a solution equation for this problem could be a subtraction problem, the structure of the problem is that of a join (change unknown) problem, which models a realistic situation where the missing value needs to be added to an initial value to create a given sum. Word problem structures such as this are examined in detail in chapter 1 of *Making Sense of Mathematics for Teaching Grades 3–5* (Dixon et al., 2016). The initial quantity is ½ of a yard, the change to the initial quantity is unknown, and the result is ⅚ of a yard. Therefore, the situation equation would be ½ + _____ = ⅚.

In the second problem, Julio needs to distribute his ½ of a pound of turkey evenly among four sandwiches. This is accomplished by further partitioning the ½ of a pound so that it is in four equal parts. You can use a rectangular drawing to illustrate this (see figure 1.11), where the large rectangle is one pound of turkey, so the shaded portion is ½ of a pound of turkey.

Now that there are four equal parts of turkey, the parts need to be named. Fractional parts are named as equal parts of a whole. In this case, the whole is the pound of turkey, or the largest rectangle in figure 1.11. Therefore, the remaining rectangle must be divided up into parts equal to the parts of turkey on each sandwich so that the amount of turkey on each sandwich can be described in terms of a fraction of a pound of turkey (see

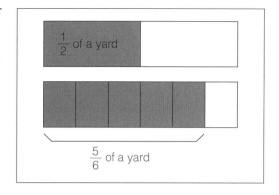

Figure 1.9: One-half yard and ⅚ yard of ribbon.

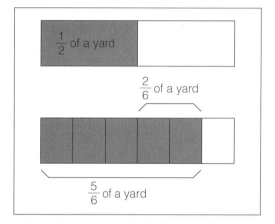

Figure 1.10: Carmen needs ²⁄₆ yard of ribbon.

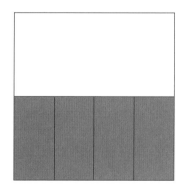

Figure 1.11: Sharing ½ pound of turkey among four sandwiches.

figure 1.12). The ½ of a pound of turkey was divided into four equal parts so the other ½ of a pound of turkey also needs to be divided into four equal parts, making eight equal parts altogether. Therefore, each sandwich will be made with ⅛ of a pound of turkey.

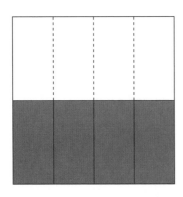

Figure 1.12: Each sandwich will have ⅛ pound of turkey.

A situation equation to model this word problem is ½ ÷ 4 = ⅛. Because ½ of a pound of turkey was shared among four sandwiches, each sandwich was made with ⅛ of a pound of turkey. There was no need to rewrite this equation as a multiplication problem to solve it. The word problem helps you make sense of fraction division. In fact, word problems can help you and your students make sense of all fraction operations if you act them out.

This context demonstrated an example of *sharing division*. When modeling sharing division, you know the total and the number of groups but you seek the number of objects in each group. The other structure for division contexts is *measurement division*. With measurement division, you know the total and how much is in each group and you seek the number of groups. (See chapter 2 of *Making Sense of Mathematics for Teaching Grades 3–5* [Dixon et al., 2016] for additional discussion of problem structures for multiplication and division.) When fractions are involved, you might not have whole groups or whole objects in groups; rather, you might have a part of a group and a part of an object. For example, if you use the same sandwich context, you would have ½ of a pound of turkey and want to know how many sandwiches you could make with ⅛ of a pound of turkey on each sandwich. This is a measurement structure because you know the total (½ of a pound of turkey), you know how much is in each group (⅛ of a pound of turkey per sandwich), and you need to determine how many groups you can make (four sandwiches).

The third problem in figure 1.8 (page 22) is solved by finding three groups of ¾ of a cup of cocoa. This problem can be drawn in several ways. It is common to draw three wholes with ¾ of each whole shaded (see figure 1.13).

Figure 1.13: Three groups of ¾ of a cup of cocoa.

Your goal is to determine how much cocoa this is altogether. One way is to count the number of fourths. This would result in 9/4 cups of cocoa. Another way is to make full cups by rearranging the fourths in the picture. You could use one fourth-size piece from the last cup to complete the first cup and another fourth-sized piece to complete the second cup. This would indicate that Ming needs two full cups and ¼ of an additional cup or 2 ¼ cups of cocoa.

The equation to represent this situation is 3 × ¾ = ⁹⁄₄ = 2 ¼. The solution equation could be represented as ¾ + ¾ + ¾ = ⁹⁄₄ = 2 ¼. This problem can be solved by multiplying a fraction by a whole number or by adding fractions with like denominators. These different strategies provide reinforcement for why these two topics are placed prior to adding fractions with unlike denominators and are in grade 4 in the learning progression.

The fourth problem in figure 1.8 (page 22) is a comparison problem, comparing the amount Blake ate (¾ of a candy bar) to the amount Jordan ate (⅝ of a candy bar). Figure 1.14 provides a visual of this comparison.

When the ¾ of a candy bar is compared to the ⅝ of a candy bar, it is clear that Blake ate part of a fourth more. Equivalent fractions are used to describe that part in terms of equal parts of the whole. If you cut each fourth into two equal pieces, you can see that the part of the fourth representing how much more Blake ate than Jordan can be described as ⅛ of a candy bar. So, Blake ate ⅛ of a candy bar more than Jordan (see figure 1.15).

An equation to represent this solution process is ¾ – ⅝ = ⅛. The process was really to change ¾ to ⁶⁄₈ so that ⁶⁄₈ – ⅝ = ⅛. By recording the steps used to solve the problem in equation form, the standard algorithm for subtracting fractions with unlike denominators begins to emerge out of sense making with word problems rather than as a set of rules to be memorized. The importance of using word problems cannot be overstated. You need to be prepared to provide word problems to your students to support sense making. It may be necessary to create word problems to support students' learning, which can sometimes be more complicated than anticipated (see figure 1.16).

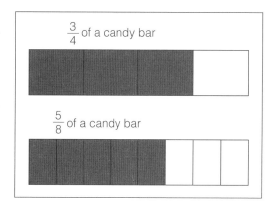

Figure 1.14: Blake's ¾ of a candy bar compared to Jordan's ⅝ of a candy bar.

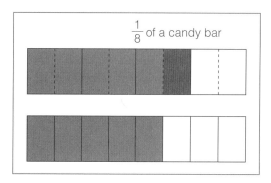

Figure 1.15: Blake ate ⅛ of a candy bar more than Jordan.

Write a word problem to support solving ⅘ – ½ that begins "Stefan had ⅘ of a pizza left over in his refrigerator . . ."

Figure 1.16: Leftover pizza task.

Did you write something like this?

> Stefan had ⅘ of a pizza left over in his refrigerator. If he ate ½ of the leftover pizza, how much pizza does he have now?

Does this word problem make sense? At first, it may seem to make sense and match the expression ⅘ – ½. Using drawings to act out the problem can provide clarity. Figure 1.17 provides this illustration.

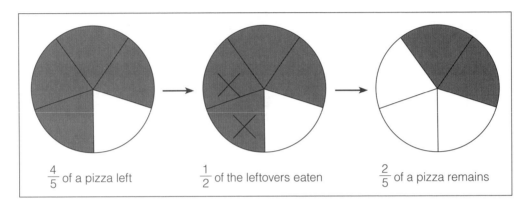

$$\frac{4}{5} \text{ of a pizza left} \qquad \frac{1}{2} \text{ of the leftovers eaten} \qquad \frac{2}{5} \text{ of a pizza remains}$$

Figure 1.17: Illustration of eating ½ of the leftover pizza.

The illustration in figure 1.17 clearly matches the word problem, but does it match the expression? Is it modeled by ⅘ – ½? Does ⅘ – ½ = ⅖? Using the algorithm to find ⅘ – ½ requires you to find common denominators. In doing so, you could represent the expression as ⁸⁄₁₀ – ⁵⁄₁₀. However, when you perform the subtraction, you see that ⁸⁄₁₀ – ⁵⁄₁₀ = ³⁄₁₀. This is a problem because ³⁄₁₀ is not the same as ⅖! The drawing leads to the result of ⅖. How could this be?

The word problem is not correctly modeled by ⅘ – ½ but rather it is modeled by ⅘ – (½ × ⅘). There is ⅘ of a pizza left over, and Stefan must eat ½ of a *whole* pizza from what is left over in order to support ⅘ – ½. A correct word problem to support ⅘ – ½ is:

> *Stefan had ⅘ of a pizza left over in his refrigerator. If he ate ½ of an entire pizza from what was left over, how much pizza does he have now?*

The wording seems strange, but it supports ⅘ – ½. The challenge is that ⅘ and ½ must refer to the same-size whole; ⅘ of an entire pizza and ½ of an entire pizza. This issue with misrepresenting fraction subtraction is common but is less likely to occur when using comparison subtraction problems, as in problem 4 in figure 1.8 (page 22). It is also less likely to occur when the unit is more clearly defined, for example when working with yards of fabric rather than with pizza. Teachers need to be intentional in their selection of tasks and include tasks of many different contexts and structures to ensure that students have the opportunity to use common errors as a springboard for learning. For an in-depth discussion of this common error, see Dixon et al. (2014).

Returning to the problems in figure 1.8 (page 22), what operation is indicated in problem 5? How do you know? This problem is a division problem. How is this problem different from problem 2? In problem 2, the amount of turkey was being shared with a whole number of sandwiches, so this modeled sharing division. In problem 5, the total amount of fabric is known, and the amount of fabric per project is known. The unknown is how many projects, or how many groups of ⅔ of a yard of fabric, can be made. To represent your thinking, you might draw a visual model like the one shown in figure 1.18.

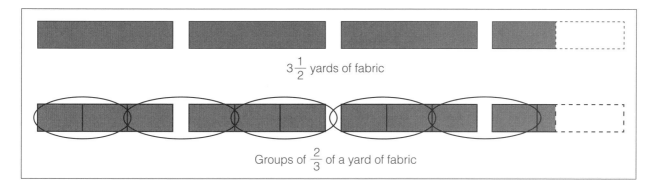

Figure 1.18: Yards of fabric divided into thirds.

The challenge now becomes to define how many projects Amanda can make. As shown in the picture, she can make five full projects. How do you describe the remaining piece of fabric? Naming fractions relies on defining equal parts of a whole. How many equal parts that are the size of the leftover piece are there in one whole yard of fabric? Using the right side of figure 1.18, you can break apart the fabric into equally sized pieces that are the same size as the leftover piece of fabric. There are six equal parts in the whole yard (see figure 1.19).

This drawing helps you see that the leftover piece of fabric is ⅙ of a yard of fabric. Recall the question you are answering: how many projects can Amanda make? Is the leftover piece the same as ⅙ of a project? How many of those pieces make one project? Two of those pieces make ⅓ of a yard, so four of them make ⅔ of a yard, or one project. Since four pieces make one project, each piece is ¼ of a project. Therefore, Amanda can make 5¼ projects. What is left to

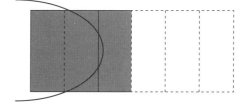

Figure 1.19: Determining the leftover piece of fabric.

be determined is which answer makes sense for the context: five projects and the remainder is ignored, or 5¼ projects and the fraction describes a part of a project that could be made with the remaining fabric. Which answer is better is not as clear and leaves some room for interpretation.

After students have made sense of fraction operations through word problems, they will benefit from additional practice solving fraction computation problems with manipulatives and drawings. This type of instruction can also be an effective use of the layers of facilitation (I facilitate the whole class, I facilitate small groups, I facilitate individuals) in the classroom. Providing opportunities for students to make sense of fraction operations through word problems can be done effectively with whole-class facilitation of initial exploration of the problems. As students are working in small groups, formative assessment can indicate where individual students may need more support and can provide a window into an effective plan for presenting strategies through whole-class facilitation. Manipulatives are useful for exploring fraction operations; however, they can also be limiting.

Using Manipulatives to Compute With Fractions

It is important that you explore fraction operations using different manipulatives, such as pattern blocks and fraction tiles. The experience will be enhanced if you actually use these manipulatives while solving the problems rather than just reading about them. We've organized the problems by manipulative to facilitate this process. Be sure to solve the problems presented in each task using the indicated manipulative prior to reading the text that follows that task.

Pattern Blocks

It will be helpful for you to explore how pattern blocks can be used to represent fractions if you have not used them in this manner in the past. Pattern blocks represent an area model for fractions and are useful when exploring operations with mixed numbers because the manipulative can represent a number of different quantities.

In this chapter, the hexagon will be used as the whole. Examine what fractional part of the whole would be represented by one triangle, one rhombus (the blue rhombus in the set, not the tan rhombus), or one trapezoid. These are the pieces that will be used in the task that follows. Use pattern blocks to model the problems in figure 1.20. If you do not have easy access to this manipulative, you can find it online at virtual manipulative sites.

Solve with pattern blocks. Use the hexagon as the whole for each problem.

1. $1\frac{1}{3} \div 2 = ?$
2. $\frac{3}{5} \times 2\frac{1}{2} = ?$
3. $3\frac{1}{3} \times \frac{1}{2} = ?$
4. $\frac{5}{6} \div 2 = ?$

Figure 1.20: Fraction operation tasks with pattern blocks.

In the first problem, you likely started with showing 1⅓ with one hexagon and one rhombus as shown in figure 1.21.

What does 1⅓ ÷ 2 mean? In this case, division by two can be interpreted as sharing between two groups. This problem could be placed in context by determining how much of a cookie each person would get if 1⅓ cookies were equally shared between two people. The hexagon and the rhombus could

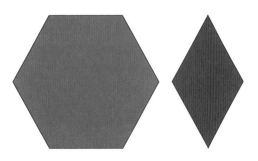

Figure 1.21: Pattern blocks showing 1⅓.

represent 1⅓ cookies. If the hexagon was split into three rhombuses, there would be four rhombuses in all, so each person would receive two of them. How much of a hexagon is this? Each person would receive ⅔ of a hexagon, or, with the context provided, ⅔ of a cookie.

The second problem, multiplying ⅗ × 2 ½, may be less straightforward. What does this fraction problem mean? Thinking of it in context will help you find meaning in the operation, which is interesting, because students are often led to believe that word problems make mathematics more difficult. In this instance, they actually make the problem easier to compute with a visual model. What could ⅗ × 2½ represent? It could represent determining how much pie is in ⅗ of 2½ pies. This context helps you realize that the first action is to represent 2½ pies. This is accomplished with two hexagons and one trapezoid. The next action is to split the 2½ pies into five equal parts so that ⅗ of the 2½ can be determined. This may be challenging at first, until you realize that the 2½ can be exchanged for five trapezoids. At this point, the solution to the problem becomes evident. Three-fifths of the five trapezoids is three trapezoids, or ³⁄₂. You can also use two of the trapezoids to make up one hexagon, or one whole, so you have 1½ as the product (see figure 1.22). This answer is reasonable because ⅗ × 2½ is approximately ½ of 3, or 1½.

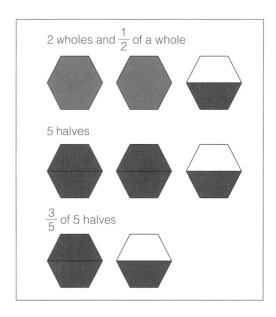

Figure 1.22: Representing ⅗ × 2½ with pattern blocks.

The third problem in figure 1.20 involves finding more than one group of ½. This problem is different from others encountered so far in this chapter. You are finding three groups of ½ and an additional ⅓ of a group of ½, or 3 and ⅓ groups of ½. Three groups of ½ can be represented with pattern blocks using three trapezoids, but how do you find ⅓ of a group of ½? One-third of a group of ½ is found by exchanging a trapezoid for three triangles and using one of them to represent ⅓ of the trapezoid. Figure 1.23 illustrates 3⅓ groups of ½ with three trapezoids and one triangle, which are then combined to make one whole and ⁴⁄₆ of another whole by exchanging two trapezoids for a hexagon and one trapezoid for three triangles.

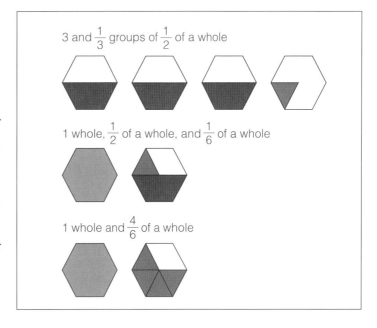

Figure 1.23: Representing 3⅓ × ½ with pattern blocks.

The final problem in figure 1.20 involves division of a fraction by a whole number. To make sense of the problem, it is helpful to represent it in context. What might be a context for this problem? A problem could be something like this:

Jeff has ⅚ of a pie. How much pie will each person get if he shares it fairly with his friend?

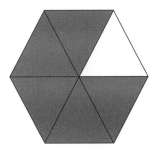

Figure 1.24: Pattern blocks representing ⅚.

Once again, the context helps to provide a starting point for representing and solving this problem visually. If the hexagon is your whole, you would begin with five triangles to represent ⅚ of the pie (see figure 1.24).

How would you share this fairly between two people? This cannot be modeled with a standard set of pattern blocks. The five sixth-sized pieces, represented by triangles, cannot be shared evenly between two people; there is not a piece that represents half of a sixth. It would seem that this problem could not be solved with pattern blocks, unless the whole was represented by more than one pattern block piece. However, consider this context:

> Jeff has ⅚ of a pie. He is supposed to bring 2 pies to the dinner party.
> What portion of what he is supposed to bring does he have?

Representing the solution process for this problem also begins with five triangles if the hexagon is the whole. Two hexagons represent the amount of pie Jeff needs to bring to the dinner party. The question

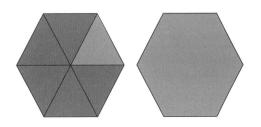

Figure 1.25: Pattern blocks representing ⅚ ÷ 2.

is answered by determining the fraction of two hexagons covered by the five triangles (see figure 1.25). The answer is 5⁄12 of the two pies. In this context, rather than sharing the ⅚ of a pie, the goal was to make a group of two pies; however, there was not enough pie to do this. There was only enough pie to make 5⁄12 of what was needed.

A slight change in thinking about the context helps make sense of the problem.

Fraction Tiles

While pattern blocks represent an area model, fraction tiles can be used to represent a linear model. For additional conversation on different fraction models see chapter 3 of *Making Sense of Mathematics for Teaching Grades 3–5* (Dixon et al., 2016). Use fraction tiles to solve the three problems in figure 1.26. These are also available online. Be sure to solve them before reading the discussion of their solutions.

Solve with fraction tiles.

1. $\frac{1}{4} + \frac{2}{3} = ?$

2. $\frac{3}{4} \times \frac{2}{3} = ?$

3. $\frac{5}{12} \div \frac{1}{6} = ?$

Figure 1.26: Fraction operations with fraction tiles task.

Fraction tiles are different from pattern blocks in that they represent a different fraction model (linear versus area) but also because the pieces are typically labeled with their fraction names. This can be helpful in connecting work with manipulatives to computing with algorithms. Figure 1.27 illustrates the process of adding the fractions in problem one. Fraction tiles for ¼ and ⅔ are laid out end to end. In order to name them as one fraction, those tiles are replaced with twelfth-size pieces because fourths and thirds can both be described as twelfths. That is, ¼ is equivalent to ³⁄₁₂ and ⅔ is equivalent to ⁸⁄₁₂. This process can be represented symbolically as ¼ + ⅔ = ³⁄₁₂ + ⁸⁄₁₂ = ¹¹⁄₁₂.

Using fraction tiles for multiplication is slightly more confusing because of how the tiles are labeled. The second problem in figure 1.26 requires you to find ¾ of the length of ⅔ of the whole. Notice the change in language to support the linear model—using the attribute

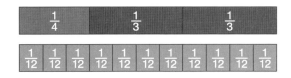

Figure 1.27: Representing ¼ + ⅔ with fraction tiles.

of length indicates that you are thinking of the manipulative as a linear model for fractions as opposed to an area model. It's important to match your language with the manipulatives you provide students. As students learn to represent fraction operations visually, the tools they have access to should connect to the context. In essence, when you are thinking about representing fraction operations in this way, *you are engaging in Mathematical Practice 5, "Use appropriate tools strategically."*

You begin with ⅔ of the length of one whole, but then you need to find ¾ of that length. This is accomplished by finding a way to partition the ⅔ into four equal lengths so that you can find ¾ of ⅔. What is confusing here is that the tiles that allow you to partition ⅔ into fourths are actually labeled as sixths because they are each ⅙ of the original whole length. Three of those pieces represent ¾ of the ⅔ and so ³⁄₆ is ¾ of the length of ⅔ of the whole, or ¾ × ⅔ = ³⁄₆, as illustrated in figure 1.28. Just as in the problems in figure 1.1 (page 16), the answer is not the expected solution from the algorithm or the answer in simplest terms but, instead, the answer that makes sense from modeling with the manipulatives.

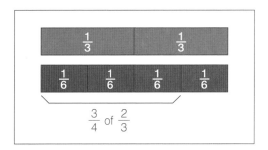

Figure 1.28: Representing ¾ × ⅔ using fraction tiles.

In the third problem in figure 1.26, the goal is to find how many lengths of ⅙ of the whole are in ⁵⁄₁₂ of the whole. This problem could be placed into context as follows:

> You have ⁵⁄₁₂ of a stick of butter. You want to make a flavored popcorn recipe that calls for ⅙ of a stick of butter for each batch. If you follow the recipe, how many batches of popcorn could you make so that you use up all the butter?

To solve this with fraction tiles, start with ⁵⁄₁₂ of the whole. Line up the ⅙-length tiles along the ⁵⁄₁₂ to see how many batches of popcorn you could make with the butter you have available, and see that you could make two batches with some butter left over (see figure 1.29).

Figure 1.29: Representing ⁵⁄₁₂ ÷ ⅙ using fraction tiles.

What remains is determining how to handle the leftover butter. It is represented by ¹⁄₁₂ of the whole stick, but does that answer the question? The question asked, "How many batches could you make so that you use up all the butter?" You could make two batches and ½ of a third batch because ¹⁄₁₂ is ½ of the amount of butter you need to make another batch. It is ½ of ⅙, therefore, ⁵⁄₁₂ ÷ ⅙ = 2½.

The confusion with what to do with the leftover amount is something encountered when using visual models to solve fraction division. It is not encountered when using algorithms to divide. This point of confusion will be discussed further in The Classroom and The Response sections later in this chapter. Now we turn our attention to developing an understanding of algorithms.

Connecting Visual Solutions to Algorithms

While manipulatives are very helpful in many situations, they can limit the fractions used in computation. As can be seen in the examples in this section, the selection of tasks needs to be intentional in order to facilitate the use of the manipulatives and link to making sense of fraction operations both in and out of context. For example, if you are using pattern blocks to add fractions, you cannot add ⅓ + ¼ while using a single block, such as the hexagon, to represent the whole. It is even more difficult to add fifths with pattern blocks. Drawings allow for more freedom in using different fractions; however, some fractions, like sevenths, can be difficult to draw. Eventually, students should compute with fractions using equations rather than visuals. Make sure you connect students' experiences with visual models to their work with procedures.

The algorithm for adding fractions with unlike denominators is fairly straightforward as long as attention is given to the language used when describing the process. For further development of addition and subtraction algorithms for fractions, see *Making Sense of Mathematics for Teaching Grades 3–5* (Dixon et al., 2016). Consider the task in figure 1.30.

Claudia ate ½ of a large cookie after lunch and then ⅓ of the cookie for a snack. How much of the large cookie did she eat?

Figure 1.30: Adding fractions using an algorithm task.

What process would you use to solve this problem using an algorithm? It is likely that you would begin by finding common denominators. What would you do next? What language would you use to describe this part of the process?

Once the amounts of cookie Claudia ate are described as ³⁄₆ and ²⁄₆, the language typically used to determine the answer to this problem goes something like, "Since the denominators are the same, you just add the numerators." Contrast this with language supportive of building conceptual understanding of the fraction addition algorithm: "Since all of the pieces are now the same size, you can combine the pieces. She ate three sixth-size pieces and two sixth-size pieces, so she ate five sixth-size pieces altogether, or ⅚ of a cookie." Using this sort of language prevents students from making the common error of adding the numerators and adding the denominators. Using a word problem, a context, helps bring meaning to the algorithm.

Problems like number 3 in figure 1.1 (page 16) provide an excellent opportunity to make similar connections between word problems and the algorithm for multiplying fractions. If students solve several problems involving the context of area with dimensions less than one whole, they can begin to see a pattern across problems. For instance, they see that the number of parts in the whole can be found by multiplying the denominators, and the shaded region can be found by multiplying the numerators. They may even begin using this line of reasoning without needing to be told. These students are engaging in Mathematical Practice 8, "Look for and express regularity in repeated reasoning."

Mathematical Practice 8 and Mathematical Practice 7, "Look for and make use of structure," are helpful for making sense of the invert and multiply algorithm for dividing fractions. Fraction division is introduced in grade 5 with division of whole numbers by unit fractions and unit fractions by whole numbers. This entryway into fraction division allows for a meaningful development of the algorithm. Consider the problem 6 ÷ ⅓. What context might support this problem? You might write a context like this:

Mr. Clark has 6 pans of brownies. He wants to make bags that each contain ⅓ of a pan of brownies for the bake sale. How many bags can he make?

This problem can be interpreted as representing the number of thirds in six wholes. Solving it with a visual model might involve drawing six rectangles and partitioning each rectangle into three equal parts for a solution of eighteen parts in all, or eighteen one-thirds (see figure 1.31).

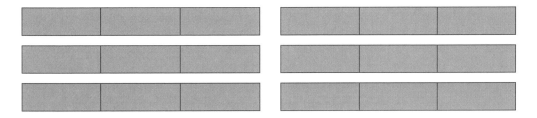

Figure 1.31: How many thirds are in six wholes?

Since each rectangle is split into three equal parts, with each part being one-third, another way of thinking about this is six groups of three one-thirds. This second way leads to the standard algorithm because you began with 6 ÷ ⅓ and changed it to 6 × 3 to describe the solution. Thus, 6 ÷ ⅓ = 6 × 3 = 18. As students explore different problems that involve division by a unit fraction, they use Mathematical Practice 8, "Look for and express regularity in repeated reasoning," to draw conclusions based on the patterns they see.

The transition from dividing whole numbers by unit fractions to dividing whole numbers by any fraction follows nicely. Suppose Mr. Clark decided to put ⅔ of a pan of brownies in each bag. How would that change the number of bags he could make? Since there are three one-thirds in each whole, you know that there are eighteen groups of ⅓ in six wholes. How can that help you determine the number of groups of ⅔ there are in six wholes? Since ⅔ is twice the size of ⅓, then there would be half as many groups of ⅔ as ⅓. Therefore, there are nine groups of ⅔ in six wholes (see figure 1.32).

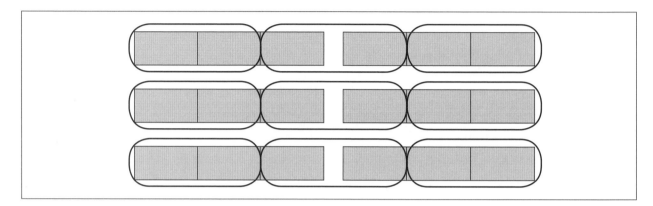

Figure 1.32: Nine groups of ⅔ in six wholes.

How does this connect to the algorithm? To find the number of one-thirds, you find 6 × 3. Then to regroup the one-thirds into groups that are ⅔ of a pan of brownies in size, you would have half as many groups. This leads to the standard algorithm by multiplying 6 × 3 and dividing by two, or finding 6 × 3/2.

The process of making sense of the algorithm to this point relies heavily on Mathematical Practice 7, "Look for and make use of structure." Extending this exploration to dividing fractions by fractions is possible but is served better by using Mathematical Practice 8, "Look for and express regularity in repeated reasoning." Students look for regularity in repeated reasoning when they use the algorithm for a wide range of division problems with both fractions and mixed numbers, and record the original expression, the expression once you invert and multiply, and the answer. They check the solutions by using drawings to see that the algorithm is applied successfully to the other situations. Connecting the algorithm to visual models supports a deeper understanding of how to determine the solution when dividing fractions.

You might be surprised to know that there is another algorithm for dividing fractions. It involves finding common denominators. What happens if both the dividend and the divisor have a common denominator? If the denominators are the same, the problem can be solved in the same manner as a whole number division problem. Once the dividend and the divisor are described as fractions with common denominators, dividing the numerators results in the quotient.

Reconsider 6 ÷ ⅔ and rewrite it as ¹⁸⁄₃ ÷ ⅔. How does this relate to the picture in figure 1.32? There are eighteen third-size pieces in six wholes. The context provided asks you to separate these eighteen pieces into sets of ⅔, or two pieces each, so this becomes eighteen pieces divided by two pieces per group, which is nine groups. Consider ⅚ ÷ ⅔. You can rewrite the expression using common denominators as ⅚ ÷ ⁴⁄₆. Now you are finding how many groups of four sixth-size pieces are in five sixth-size pieces, or how many groups of four are in five. There is one group of four pieces and ¼ of another group, or 1¼ groups as illustrated in figure 1.33.

This algorithm might actually become your preferred algorithm, because it is more readily justified with both fractions and mixed numbers. What is important is that students can justify the processes they use when operating with fractions. The same is true for operations with integers.

Making Sense of Integers

How were you taught to add, subtract, multiply, and divide integers? Did you make sense of the procedures, or did you just memorize them? How do you teach them now? Often, just like with fractions, processes for integer operations are introduced as a set of rules to be memorized. This is not consistent with understanding integer operations with depth or with the position we take in this book. Rather, students should make sense of processes for integer operations, and conceptual understanding should precede a focus on procedures.

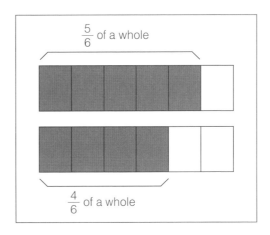

Figure 1.33: One group of four sixth-size pieces and ¼ of a group of four sixth-size pieces in ⅚.

Conceptual understanding of integers is established when integers are introduced and operated upon in context. Michelle Stephan (2009) provides an instructional sequence that involves introducing integers in terms of assets and debts. Students use this context and tasks related to it to *invent* rules for integer operations. What scenarios come to mind when you think of assets and debts?

Stephan (2009) uses the net worth of famous people. For the purpose of this discussion, fictitious people will be used; however, with students, using a person of interest to them may be more motivating. This also helps students make sense of the terms involved with this activity, including *assets, debts, loans,* and *investment.* Ida Famous will serve as the first famous person for this discussion. Ida has a net worth of $50,000,000. How is her net worth determined? It is determined by combining her assets and her debts. This is where the context supports positive and negative values. In order to determine Ida's net worth, students can brainstorm a list of potential assets and debts. Assets are described as positive numbers, and debts are negative.

The net values of different people can be compared and represented on a number line. A *vertical* number line is used, as it is often more intuitive to students. There is less confusion regarding where negative numbers are placed relative to the location of zero. Use a vertical number line to complete the problem in figure 1.34.

Represent the net worth of each of the following fictitious people on a vertical number line then answer the questions that follow.

Name:	Net Worth:
Notta Saver	−$100,000
Rich R. Thanu	$700,000
Ida Spendit	−$300,000
E. Van Steven	$0

Who has the greatest net worth? Who has the least? How much is the net worth of the person with the least net worth compared to the person with the greatest net worth?

Figure 1.34: Comparing net worth with a vertical number line task.

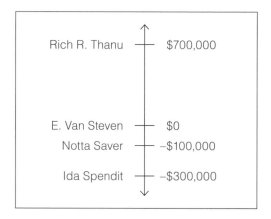

Figure 1.35: A vertical number line for net worth.

How did you use the number line? It is likely that you placed the zero first and then recorded the other values. In doing so, you were focusing on the other numbers' values relative to zero. This is helpful when making sense of integers. Figure 1.35 provides an example of a vertical number line with each net worth labeled.

Notice that the vertical number line in figure 1.35 is an *open number line* in that other numbers are not included and proportion is not maintained. It is used to organize thinking about placement of integers and for making sense of operations with integers. Using the vertical number line, it becomes obvious that Rich R. Thanu has the greatest net worth and Ida Spendit has the least. In answering the problem comparing the net worth of Rich and Ida, you see that Ida is worth $1,000,000 less than Rich. How might you describe that using integers? You might say that Ida's net worth is –$1,000,000 compared to Rich's net worth. While the *difference* is –1,000,000, the *distance* between the values is 1,000,000. This provides an excellent opportunity to discuss the meaning of absolute value in context.

Using transactions with assets and debts helps students formalize operations with integers. Reconsider the characters from the task in figure 1.34 (page 35). What if Rich started spending too much money, Notta also spent more but then started making money, and Ida continued to spend? How might you keep track of their net worth? Consider the net worth transactions task in figure 1.36 and record your thinking on vertical number lines.

What is the new net worth? Make sense of the following scenarios using a vertical number line.

1. Rich began with a net worth of $700,000 but then made a very bad investment and lost $900,000. What is his new net worth?

2. Notta began with a net worth of –$100,000 and then got a loan for $400,000 and spent the money so she could start a business writing screenplays.

    a. What is her new net worth?

    b. Once Notta got her business underway, she sold six different screenplays for $200,000 each. What was her new net worth?

3. Ida began with a net worth of –$300,000. Her quadruplets were ready to start law school. She took out 4 loans at $100,000 each so she could lend the money to each of her four daughters so they could attend law school. What was her new net worth?

Figure 1.36: Net worth transactions task.

How did you represent the transactions? Did you record the transactions in one jump, or did you make a series of jumps? When the transaction causes the result to go from positive to negative or negative to positive, it is common to jump to the zero point on the number line and then to jump the rest of the way. Figure 1.37 provides an example of how the first problem in figure 1.36 could have been solved on the number line.

How would you use a situation equation to model the transaction? Rich began with $700,000 then lost $900,000 for a result of −$200,000. The equation could be 700,000 − 900,000 = −200,000. But what if you thought of the situation as adding more debt? Since debt is described as a negative value, the situation would be modeled as 700,000 + (−900,000) = −200,000. Having these sorts of conversations with students helps them develop a flexible and deep understanding of operations with integers.

The second problem describes a transaction that starts with a negative that becomes more negative as Notta adds more debt to her net worth. How did you represent this with a vertical number line? Figure 1.38 provides one way to illustrate this. Notice how the transaction is shown with just one jump. This transaction is more likely to be represented with one jump because it does not cross zero.

How did you represent Notta's new net worth in the second problem with a situation equation? Did you think of this as subtracting assets or adding debt? Either approach is correct in this context and, again, provides a useful talking point with students as they develop rules for adding and subtracting positive and negative numbers. You could have modeled this situation with either −100,000 − 400,000 = −500,000 or −100,000 + −400,000 = −500,000.

In part b of the second problem of figure 1.36, Notta improves her net worth substantially. She adds six positive transactions. How did you represent this on the number line? Figure 1.39 provides an illustration of one way to represent this using six jumps of $200,000 in the positive direction.

Modeling groups of numbers is accomplished with multiplication. Since Notta began with a net worth of −$500,000, the situation equation would be −500,000 + 6(200,000) = 700,000. This process combines multiplying positive numbers with adding a positive value to a negative value.

The last situation in the task in figure 1.36 provides an opportunity to explore multiplying a positive times a negative. In this last problem, Ida begins at −$300,000 but then increases her debt as she takes four loans of $100,000 each. How did you represent this on a vertical number line? Compare your representation to the one provided in figure 1.40 (page 38).

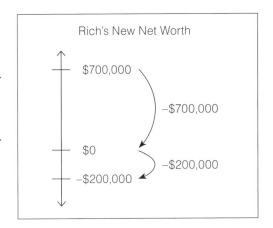

Figure 1.37: Using a vertical number line to show Rich's new net worth.

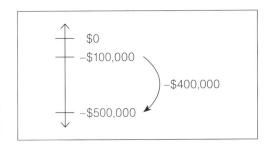

Figure 1.38: Using a vertical number line to show adding debt to debt—Notta's new net worth (part a).

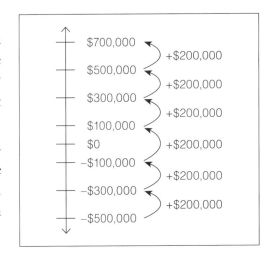

Figure 1.39: Jumping six groups of +$200,000 on a vertical number line—Ida's new net worth.

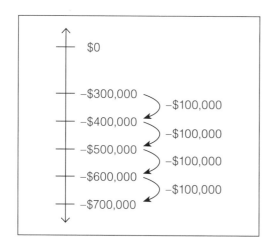

Figure 1.40: Jumping four groups of –$100,000 on a vertical number line—Ida's new net worth.

The situation equation for Ida's transaction would be –300,000 + 4(–100,000) = –700,000. The context allowed you to make sense of multiplying a positive number times a negative quantity. The vertical number line supported the sense making as it was used to illustrate moving in the negative direction four times. Experiences such as these provide opportunities to engage students in Mathematical Practice 4, "Model with mathematics." You mathematized the four situations provided in figure 1.36 (page 36) using both the vertical number line and situation equations. You are encouraged to provide similar opportunities for your students.

Once students have explored modeling with mathematics as described through the use of tasks similar to those in figure 1.36, they should be supported to engage in Mathematical Practice 8, "Look for and express regularity in repeated reasoning," to develop the rules for operating with integers. Students can create tables with the situation equations and then write descriptions of what they notice with respect to commonalities and differences across problems. In this way, the procedures for operating with integers are based on conceptual understanding so that if students forget the rules they develop, they can use the understanding they have of the concepts to make sense of a problem.

What is critical in this process is for students to use strategies that are accurate, efficient, and generalizable. Students must be able to explain *and* justify the algorithms they use. This is important for you as well so that you can support students during instruction. If given the opportunity, students should be able to make sense of fraction operations and integer concepts and operations. The videos described next provide a window into what this looks like in the classroom.

The Classroom

Now that you have made sense of fraction operations, think about what instruction looks like when the focus is on developing conceptual understanding of operations with fractions. The following videos provide opportunities to observe students in action doing the sense making.

The first video offers a window into a sixth-grade class where students explore dividing a mixed number by a fraction. Prior to watching the first video, solve the task in figure 1.41.

Douglas ordered 5 small pizzas during the great pizza sale. He ate ⅙ of one pizza and wants to freeze the remaining 4⅚ pizzas. Douglas decides to freeze the remaining pizza in serving-size bags. A serving of pizza is ⅔ of a pizza. How many servings can he make if he uses up all the pizza?

Figure 1.41: Leftover pizza task.

What did you get as an answer? It is likely that you determined that Douglas could make 7⅙ servings or 7¼ servings. Which answer is correct? This is the topic of discussion in the sixth-grade class. Watch the first video before proceeding.

www.solution-tree.com/Dividing_Fractions_in_Context

Notice how the students are given time to make sense of the problem in ways that they choose. Some students draw pictures, and others use manipulatives. One student in particular draws circles to represent the pizza—this student chooses a model that is consistent with the context as discussed earlier. It is interesting that the student divides one circle into sixths and the others into thirds. This student is not simply following a procedure but rather acting out the context of the problem as part of the solution process with drawings. The students who use pattern blocks also rely on the context to attempt to make sense of the problem when they are making sets of two-thirds but don't use up all the thirds in each whole.

The context is helpful in making sense of the problem but also leads to errors with the problem as students try to determine what to do with the remainder. This is an error that would likely not be encountered if students were strictly using procedures to divide fractions, and teachers must be prepared to address this when teaching fraction operations conceptually.

The second video is of a fifth-grade class focusing on multiplying fractions. The teacher in this video is prepared to address student errors that occur during instruction. Prior to watching the second video, it might make sense for you to solve the task in the video (see figure 1.42) using a visual model so that you can compare the process you used to how the class solves the problem. The students use a fraction kit as a visual to model the problem. Fraction kits are discussed in chapters 3 and 4 of *Making Sense of Mathematics for Teaching Grades 3–5* (Dixon et al., 2016).

Solve the following using a visual model.

Suzie had ¼ of a pan of brownies. She ate ¾ of what she had. How much of the original pan of brownies did Suzie eat?

Figure 1.42: Fifth-grade video task.

What did you use to represent the pan of brownies? It is likely that you used a rectangular shape as that is the shape of most brownie pans. How did you name the three-fourths of the one-fourth of the pan using fraction language? Perhaps you saw that they were sixteenths of the entire pan of brownies. How might this be handled in the classroom? Take note of how the teacher uses the fraction kit to help the students make sense of naming fractions. Watch the second video before proceeding.

www.solution-tree.com/Multiplying_Fractions_Using
_a_Fraction_Kit

The teacher identifies the red piece of paper from the fraction kit as the whole to remove unnecessary confusion regarding representing the problem. This is so the focus remains on how to find parts of a fourth. In this way, the students can focus on finding fourths of a fourth and naming them. The students are able to use the green pieces to show three-fourths of the original fourth-size piece. The difficulty is in naming those pieces in terms of the whole. This is an aspect of fraction operations that is new to fifth-grade students as they begin to make sense of fraction multiplication. The teacher anticipates this and is prepared to provide scaffolding as necessary. The teacher is planning and teaching with common errors in mind.

A goal of this lesson is for students to do the sense making with a problem type that is new to them. Notice how the teacher begins the process of the *layers of facilitation* by supporting the entire class to solve the problem as opposed to modeling the solution process for them. Who makes sense of the problem? How is support provided when students struggle?

The teacher begins this lesson by asking students to describe what happens first in the problem. He then uses the fraction kit to help students see how it can represent the context of the problem. Once a common way of representing the pan of brownies and ¼ of the pan is established, he again returns the thinking and sense making to the students so that they can use the context of the problem to determine what to do next.

When it seems that students struggle with how to use the fraction kit to determine ¾ of the ¼ of the pan of brownies, how does the teacher respond? At this point, he facilitates the students to continue to solve the problem in small groups. Once groups have an opportunity to discuss the problem, he again asks the class how to proceed. One of the students answers but rather than closing the lesson at this point, the teacher asks another student to repeat the original student's answer. What does he do when the second student struggles?

When the student struggles, he calls on another student to provide support. This student is able to help the struggling learner. The teacher is able to check for understanding by asking the student who struggles to talk through the entire solution process to be sure that she is not simply repeating the words of the student who supported her. The teacher is facilitating the student to engage in Mathematical Practice 1, "Make sense of problems and persevere in solving them." All too often, when students struggle, teachers solve the problem for the students. Notice how, in this case, the teacher uses other students and appropriate scaffolding to help a struggling student make sense of the problem and persevere.

TQE Process

At this point, it may be helpful to watch the first video again (page 39) and pay close attention to the tasks, questioning, and opportunities to collect evidence of student learning. The TQE process can help you frame your observations. Teachers who have a deep understanding of the mathematics they teach:

- Select appropriate *tasks* to support identified learning goals

- Facilitate productive *questioning* during instruction to engage students in Mathematical Practices

- Collect and use student *evidence* in the formative assessment process during instruction

The *task* chosen for this lesson supports students to make sense of fraction division, particularly when remainders are involved. In choosing this task, the teacher is aware of potential misconceptions regarding naming the portion remaining from fraction division. Some students correctly name the piece left over, while others name it incorrectly. This task is purposefully designed to allow for this discrepancy so that students have the opportunity to make sense of which result is correct and why. The task creates dissonance among the students, and they are able to examine each other's thinking to see that the proper name of the leftover piece relies on the size of the serving created, thus engaging in Mathematical Practice 3, "Construct viable arguments and critique the reasoning of others."

The teacher uses *questioning* to gather information regarding how students are making sense of the problem. The teacher circulates the room, asking questions and listening to responses but not indicating correctness of the responses. She encourages interactions at the small-group level. She provides scaffolding as necessary, and she collects information to use later during the whole-class discussion. The teacher is looking for common errors as well as for students who solve the problem correctly. She anticipates the common errors and has plans for how to address them. As she identifies which students display the common errors, the teacher knows how to address those errors with the class during whole-group discussion.

The teacher begins the whole-class discussion by providing the two responses she heard from the class. At this point, the teacher does not indicate which response is correct. She is engaging the students in Mathematical Practice 3, "Construct viable arguments and critique the reasoning of others." If she had indicated which was correct, *she* would have been engaging in this practice rather than the students. The students defend their responses, and classmates critique one another's reasoning, unpacking a common error with fraction division in a much more impactful way than having the teacher correct the students. Notice, too, the teacher is intentional in allowing the student with the misconception to explain his thinking first. What would have happened if the group who solved it correctly explained their reasoning first? There would not have been as much engagement in the Mathematical Practice. Because the teacher was aware of the misconception and used questioning to identify which groups solved the problem in which way, she was able to sequence the classroom discussion in a meaningful and productive way.

The teacher collects *evidence* of student learning through the formative assessment process. Consider the small-group interactions, particularly the group of students using pattern blocks to represent the problem. Initially, the teacher uses formative assessment to determine that the students are not accounting for all the pizza. As the teacher asks questions of the students, she is able to support their sense making and help them account for all the pizza. As the teacher continues to circulate among the groups, she uses the formative assessment process to collect evidence that students were determining both $7\frac{1}{4}$ and $7\frac{1}{6}$ servings as possible answers. This evidence of student learning (or student misconceptions) then fuels the whole-class discussion in asking students to justify both answers and to make sense of why $7\frac{1}{4}$ servings is the correct solution as well as working to support student engagement in Mathematical Practice 6, "Attend to precision."

The Response

Typical areas of difficulty related to fraction operations occur when students use algorithms incorrectly. For example, some students may add numerators as well as denominators when adding fractions; others might forget to invert when dividing fractions. These types of errors are related to procedural memory. When a more conceptual approach is taken with instruction on fraction operations, the errors students make are impacted. The errors themselves are more conceptually based. Consider the multiple choice options presented in figure 1.43.

DO NOW

Divide.

$$1\frac{5}{6} \div \frac{1}{3}$$

a) $\frac{6}{33}$ b) $\frac{11}{18}$

c) $5\frac{1}{6}$ d) $5\frac{1}{2}$

Figure 1.43: Multiple choices showing common errors with fraction division.

The correct answer is choice d. What common errors are identified by the other choices? Options a and b represent common procedural errors of inverting the wrong fraction and forgetting to invert. Choice c does not represent an error that is common to students who are taught procedurally; this is more of a conceptual error. It is more clearly recognized by using manipulatives or drawings to represent the problem as illustrated in figure 1.44.

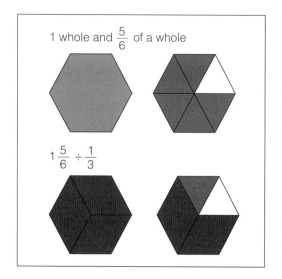

Figure 1.44: Dividing 1⅚ ÷ ⅓ conceptually with pattern blocks.

Students see that there are five groups of ⅓ of a whole in 1⅚, with ⅙ of a whole left over. These students incorrectly determine that 1⅚ ÷ ⅓ is equal to 5 ⅙. They do this because they lose track of the meaning of division as finding the number of groups when the total and the group size are known. The answer should be given in terms of the group size. In this case, there are 5 ½ groups of ⅓ in 1⅚ rather than 5 ⅙ groups.

What is an appropriate response to this sort of error? What is an intervention? For errors like this, students may need to revisit the meaning of division. They should connect what they are doing involving operations with fractions to operations with whole numbers through the use of context. You might ask students to create a context to model the problem in order to help them make sense of the remainder. When operating with fractions, focus should be placed on keeping track of the whole. In the previous example, a word problem might shed light on the errors. This problem could be placed in the context of servings of pizza.

> There are 1⅚ pizzas left over from a party, and a serving of pizza is ⅓ of a pizza. How many servings are left over?

There are 5 servings and ⅙ of a pizza left. This is 5 ½ servings, so 1⅚ ÷ ⅓ = 5 ½.

Also important in instruction and during intervention is allowing students to make sense of the operations, often through the use of manipulatives, visual models, and context. It is important to give students choices related to what manipulative or visual they use. This allows them to engage in Mathematical Practice 5, "Use appropriate tools strategically." If you determine what manipulative students should use, the students are less able to make connections for themselves and are less likely to make sense of the content at hand. It is important for students to select and use the tools themselves. It is often more time efficient to model the use of manipulatives and other tools with students; however, this limits the students making sense of the mathematics for themselves. Therefore, the saving of time is short lived. It is best to provide students access to a variety of tools and give them the opportunity to select what makes sense to them. This also supports students to realize some manipulatives and drawings are less efficient and even impossible to use with given contexts or problems, helping students to understand the aspect of strategic choice in tool use.

What is important to note is that the response to errors does not focus on rote memorization or practicing procedures exclusively. The response also includes making connections to earlier work with whole numbers to further develop an understanding of the operations—in this case, fraction operations. This is in contrast to interventions that consist of fraction computation problems devoid of context for students to perform. Practice is still important, but students often practice poorly understood procedures and sometimes even incorrect procedures when a focus on conceptual understanding is not included in the intervention. As you consider the prior knowledge for success with fraction operations and integer concepts and operations, you will find that understanding whole number operations is critical for both. Students who have difficulty recognizing how to name the remaining fraction resulting from division may have misconceptions related to naming fractions in general. Students who have difficulty with integer operations may be overgeneralizing rules or not recognizing how operations with negative numbers are different from operations with positive numbers. Bringing students back to meaningful contexts can be an effective way to provide meaningful intervention and to move learning forward.

Reflections

1. What do you feel are the key points in this chapter?

2. What challenges might you face when implementing the key ideas from this chapter? How will you overcome them?

3. What are the important features for developing an understanding of fraction operations and integer concepts and operations, and how will you ensure your instruction embeds the support needed for these features?

4. Select a recent lesson you have taught or observed focused on fractions or integers. Relate this lesson to the TQE process.

5. What changes will you make to your planning and instruction based on what you read and considered from this chapter?

CHAPTER 2

Ratios and Proportional Relationships

This chapter transitions the focus on rational numbers in terms of fractions to rational numbers as ratios and proportions. A fraction is a rational number because it describes a ratio of two numbers. In a fraction $^a/_b$, the numerator, a, describes the number of equal-size pieces of the whole, and the denominator, b (where b is not equal to 0), indicates the number of those pieces needed to make the whole. A rational number that is *not* a fraction can also be described as $^a/_b$; however, a and b ($b \neq 0$) do not describe a part-to-whole relationship. While the focus of rational numbers was on fractions in the previous chapter, ratios are explored in this chapter.

Comprehending ratio and proportionality concepts empowers students to solve problems that include a number of different real-world applications. In providing problems to solve involving ratios and proportions, you support students to develop *proportional reasoning* (Kilpatrick et al., 2001). Proportional reasoning includes the understanding of the interrelationship of two quantities and how a change in one connects to a change in the other.

The Challenge

The initial task in this chapter (see figure 2.1) provides an opportunity to apply proportional reasoning in a real-world context. Take a moment to complete the task before continuing on.

A restaurant was set up in two sections to accommodate different parties. In one section of the restaurant, there was a party of 18 people and there were enough seats for 34 people. At the same time, the other section of the restaurant had 14 people with seats for 30. Which section was more crowded? How do you know?

Figure 2.1: Crowded restaurant task.

How did you make sense of this task? What type of solution process did you use—numerical or pictorial? As you examine this task, you might notice that each section has sixteen empty seats. Does this mean that the sections are equally crowded? Why, or why not? How does each seat count toward crowdedness? The first section has more people but also more seats. How does this information affect crowdedness? Consider the representation in figure 2.2 (page 46).

The ratio of people to seats in the first section is 18:34, and the second section has a ratio of 14:30. More than half the seats are filled in section one, while less than half of the seats are filled in section two. Based on this, you might conclude that section one is more crowded. What are the ratios of filled seats to empty seats? Section one has a ratio of 18:16, and section two has a ratio of 14:16. In section one, there are more filled seats than empty, so it is more full. This type of thinking is critical as students in the middle grades transition from absolute thinking (for example, section one is more crowded because eighteen people is more than fourteen people) to relative thinking (for example, section one is more crowded because it is more than half full).

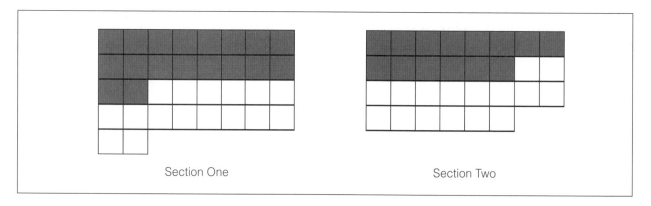

Section One   Section Two

Figure 2.2: Visual of each section of the restaurant.

Another consideration is with which Mathematical Practice did you engage as you completed the task? You most likely focused on Mathematical Practice 1, "Make sense of problems and persevere in solving them." You analyzed the given information, made a plan to solve the word problem, and then considered the reasonableness of your answer. You also might have engaged in some productive struggle if you have not solved a problem like this in the past. You also engaged in Mathematical Practice 2, "Reason abstractly and quantitatively." You used the information in the word problem to make sense of and represent the mathematical relationship in the task. Doing so allowed you to attend to the meanings of the quantities and the units in the problem to help you make sense of the problem and the solution, not just solve the problem using a procedure.

The Progression

Ratios and proportional relationships provide a mathematical link between a deep understanding of number in elementary school and the abstract reasoning processes of high school. Students begin making sense of this topic in middle school by building an understanding of ratios and unit rate. From that foundation, they use equivalent ratios to transition to making sense of proportions and apply that understanding to solve multistep problems involving proportional relationships. The following progression provides an overview of the content of ratios and proportional relationships in the middle grades, with the realization that deep understanding develops over time.

- Explore and understand ratio as a relationship between two quantities.

- Explore and understand unit rate.

- Solve ratio problems.

- Solve real-world problems involving ratios using various representations, including tables, number lines, and bar models.

- Make sense of proportional relationships.

- Determine if two quantities are proportional.

- Solve problems involving proportional relationships.

- Graph and interpret proportional relationships.

Grade 6

Reasoning with ratios in grade 6 begins with a focus on ratios as a general comparison involving two different quantities. This builds on earlier understandings around multiplication, division, and fractions. Ratio problems also include determining the unit rate as a relationship of an amount of a first quantity to one unit of a second quantity. For example, if a mixture in science is described as 8 grams of salt to 4 ounces of water, the ratio is 8 grams to 4 ounces, which is the same as 2 grams for every ounce, or the unit rate of 2 grams of salt per 1 ounce of water. This process can be shown numerically as $\frac{8}{4} = \frac{2}{1} = 2$. The unit rate is important because it supports the understanding of equivalent ratios, the advantage of making comparisons, and the ability to solve problems.

Students also learn about percent in grade 6, which is a quantity represented as a ratio out of 100. Students solve problems including finding the whole when given a part of the whole and the percent, such as finding the number of students in a class if eleven students make up 50 percent of the class. Students determine equivalent relationships involving ratios as well as reason with a constant value that is multiplied or divided between each of the ratio pairs in tables, bar models, double number line diagrams, equations, and graphs.

Grade 7

Students in grade 7 expand their understanding of ratio as a way to analyze proportional relationships and direct variation (equations of the form $y = kx$) and use these understandings to solve problems. Students expand their understanding of unit rate to include computations that include ratios of fractions, such as determining that a person who walks ¼ of a mile in ½ of an hour can be described as walking ½ of a mile per hour.

Students explore proportional reasoning in grade 7, including distinguishing proportional relationships from nonproportional relationships, in equations, tables, and graphs. Students build on their understanding of unit rate in tables and graphs, as well as with equations, diagrams, and verbal descriptions. Finally, students investigate proportional relationships to solve multistep ratio and percent problems.

Working with ratios and proportions in the middle grades encompasses understanding a wide range of rational number concepts and procedures. Proportional reasoning requires students to process changes between two quantities simultaneously and then use the relationship to solve problems. While conceptual understanding and procedural skill are both important, the development of ratio and proportional reasoning is much more likely to occur if conceptual understanding precedes a focus on computational procedures.

Grade 8

Proportional relationships are used to make sense of graphs in grade 8, linking unit rate to the slope of the graph. This connection is examined in multiple representations and includes extending how proportions are embedded in linear relationships. Ultimately, situations explored in the middle grades that require multiplicative or proportional reasoning underpin the algebra and geometry concepts explored in high school.

The Mathematics

Students in grades 6–8 extend what they have learned about multiplication and division to solve problems involving ratios and rates. The reasoning involved in making sense of and using ratios and proportions provides important groundwork for later work with linear equations and functional relationships. As students deepen their understanding of rational numbers, they learn how to distinguish fractions from other ratios, model proportional relationships, explore varied proportional problem types, use proportions to solve percent problems, develop proportional reasoning procedures, and identify proportional relationships.

Distinguishing Fractions From Ratios

In order to explore the relationship between fractions and ratios, consider how you think about the comparison task in figure 2.3.

Patricia wonders if her mathematics class or her science class has more left-handed students. After asking the students in each class, she arrives at the following results. Using Patricia's results, which class has more left-handed students?

- Her mathematics class has 24 students; 12 are left-handed.
- Her science class has 28 students; 13 are left-handed.

Figure 2.3: Left-handed students comparison task.

How did you reason about the task? What type of relationships did you consider? Did you think about the number of left-handed students, the fraction of students who are left-handed, or how many students are left-handed compared to right-handed? As with the opening task in figure 2.1 (page 45), you may have thought about this task in either absolute terms or relative terms. In absolute terms, you noticed there are 12 left-handed students in her mathematics class and 13 left-handed students in her science class. Therefore, there are more left-handed students in her science class because 13 is greater than 12.

In relative terms, you might think of the *fraction* of students who are left-handed compared to the total number of students in the class, which is a *part-to-whole relationship*. Another relation would be to think of the *ratio* of the number of students who are left-handed compared to the number of students who are right-handed, which is a *part-to-part relationship*. In the part-to-whole relationship, you may reason that exactly half of the 24 students are left-handed in Patricia's mathematics class (12), while less than half of the 28 students are left-handed in her science class (13), so, relatively, there are more left-handed students in her mathematics class. In part-to-part thinking, you would see that in Patricia's mathematics class, the ratio of left-handed students to right-handed students is 12:12, while the ratio is 13:15 in her science class. Part-to-part reasoning allows you to think that the ratio of 12:12 is greater than 13:15, because the ratio of 12:12 is the same as 1:1, while 13:15 is less than 1:1. Note that ratios can be either part-to-part or part-to-whole relationships. Fractions always represent part-to-whole relationships. Based on the context, you may have chosen the part-to-whole approach to align to comparing the number of left-handed students to the entire class. As students progress through middle-grades mathematics, both absolute and relative thinking are important in relating quantities to one another.

Modeling Proportional Relationships

Representations that show proportional reasoning include drawings or diagrams, bar models, double number lines, ratio tables, and graphs. It is likely that you prefer one representation over the others; however, it is important for you to use and understand other representations as well. Making connections between these representations is an important element in understanding proportional relationships. When students represent concepts in multiple ways and connect those representations together, they are more likely to model and communicate their mathematical thinking successfully. How would you represent your thinking about the mathematical situation described in figure 2.4?

Lily drives 90 miles in 2 hours. If she drives at the same rate, how far does Lily travel in each of the following time intervals?

   a. 1 hour

   b. ½ hour

   c. 3 hours

Figure 2.4: Driving rate task.

How can you model this relationship? Is there an advantage to using one representation over others? To foster the ability of your students to make sense of problems, you need to practice the flexibility to think about different representations of problems. Before reading on, attempt to create each of the representations listed previously and explore the different mathematical aspects that each demonstrates.

Bar Model

In order to use the bar model, you must decide what the bars should represent from the context of the given relationship. In making these decisions, you are showing your thinking and how you understand the mathematical relationship. For example, how could you use the bars to model the rate from the problem and to respond to the first part of the task? One way this could be accomplished is shown in figure 2.5.

In this model, you see one long bar shaded dark gray representing 90 miles and two short white bars representing 45 miles each. The model illustrates 90 miles in 2 hours using one dark grey bar and the rate of 45 miles per hour using one white bar. When you compare one quantity to one unit of a second quantity, you are determining the *unit rate* for the problem. Unit rates are helpful in solving problems as well as comparing rates to one another. When

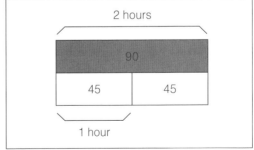

Figure 2.5: Bar model representing the relationship of 90 miles in two hours and 45 miles in one hour.

looking at this bar model, you see that the relationship of 90 miles in 2 hours can also be expressed as 45 miles in 1 hour, the unit rate.

How could you use the bar model in figure 2.5 (page 49) to help you think about the other two parts of the task? Bar models could also be used to model the distance traveled for these two time intervals (see figure 2.6).

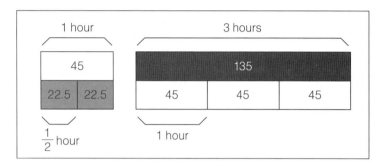

Figure 2.6: Determining how many miles Lily traveled in ½ hour and 3 hours.

Since you know one white bar represents the distance that Lily travels in 1 hour, you can use that information to solve for the other parts of the task. In order to do so, you can use the proportional relationship between the white bar and the other bars you need to create. For example, in figure 2.6, the light gray bar is shown to be half of the white bar to represent ½ hour. The proportional relationship between hours and miles allows you to determine that the light gray bar also represents half of 45 miles, or 22.5 miles. Therefore, Lily travels 22.5 miles in a ½ hour. Similarly, the black bar represents three times the span covered by one hour and therefore represents three times the distance of 45 miles. This gives the ratio 135 miles in 3 hours.

The bar model can be helpful in understanding ratio tasks as it supports you to visualize how the quantities relate to one another. The bar model allows you to compare proportional relationships, and you can show unit rate and equivalent ratios in a visual manner. Students may benefit from seeing the quantities expressed as lengths, with the size of the bars allowing them to compare ratios and develop equivalent ratios as they represent the context of the problem. Being able to divide the bars, or include multiple copies of the bars, allows them to see equivalent relationships.

Double Number Line

Another visual representation that can be used to record your proportional reasoning is a double number line. How can you show two quantities simultaneously using number lines? Initially, you need to

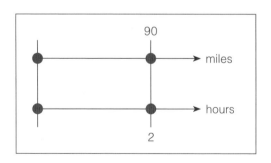

Figure 2.7: Double number line representing relationship of 90 miles in 2 hours.

decide how to express the relationship on each of two number lines, with the values of one quantity matching up to the values of the other quantity to reflect the relationship in the situation. That is, the number lines show the given information and align to form the relationships from the problem. For example, in modeling the situation in the driving rate task in figure 2.4 (page 49), your representation should show miles on one number line matched with hours on the second number line, at a rate of 90 miles in 2 hours (see figure 2.7).

In the representation, you can see the number lines coordinate the number of hours and the number of miles through the relationship of 90 miles in 2 hours. However, the representation still has not included your coordination of distance in miles for the other points in time. How can you use reasoning to determine the corresponding miles for the hours of travel on the number line shown in figure 2.8?

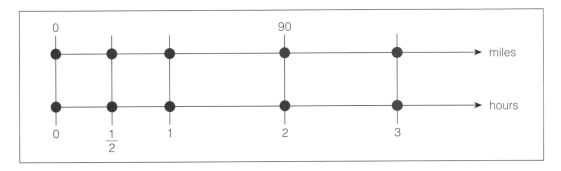

Figure 2.8: Representing various distances on a double number line.

What did you do first? It is likely that you found the unit rate by applying the fact that one is half of two so half of the distance between the zero point and 90 miles is 45 miles. This same strategy can be applied to determine the corresponding distance traveled in a ½ hour. How could you determine the distance traveled in 3 hours? You could have built on from 2 hours, adding the distance traveled in 1 hour to the distance traveled in 2 hours. You also could have iterated, or repeated, the distance traveled in 1 hour to get to 3 hours. Figure 2.9 displays these relationships.

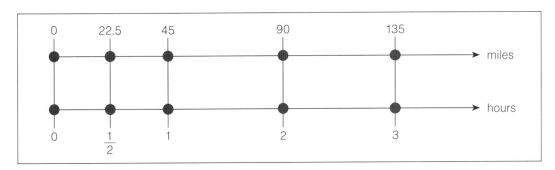

Figure 2.9: Various distances on a double number line.

The double number line allows you to show the relationship between the two quantities in a linear fashion, representing the given relationship as the same distance along two number lines. If you created your double number line on paper, you may have discovered that you can fold your paper to demonstrate the relationship of the unit rate and the relationship that included ½ hour. Such paper folding is similar to activities that students may experience in the elementary grades involving fractions and number lines. This use of number lines is described in chapter 3 of *Making Sense of Mathematics for Teaching Grades 3–5* (Dixon et al., 2016). The double number line also shows the relationship along a continuous band, implying that all values are possible along the number lines. Double number lines may not be an appropriate representation if one of the quantities in the situation can only be expressed using certain values, such as the number of buses needed to take students on a field trip, as you would need a whole number as part of the ratio.

Ratio Table

How could you express the relationship using a table? Your table might start like the table in figure 2.10. The given relationship of 90 miles in 2 hours as well as equivalent ratios can be included in the table. How can you use strategies based in proportional reasoning to determine other ratios from the task in figure 2.4 (page 49) to complete the table?

Miles	90			
Hours	2			

Figure 2.10: Ratio table representing 90 miles in 2 hours.

When exploring a set of ratios in a table, you can demonstrate your reasoning in two ways. What is the relationship between 90 miles and 2 hours? You might see it as 90 is 2 times 45, or that 90 divided by 2 is 45. In this way, you are using the relationship *within* the ratio to determine how to complete the table. In this task, dividing 90 by 2 gives you the unit rate of 45 miles per hour, which is the answer for the first part of the task. You can determine other equivalent ratios by multiplying or dividing each part of the pair of values in the ratio table by the same factor. For example, you could multiply each part of the unit rate in the table by 3 or by ½ and as a result determine equivalent ratios (see figure 2.11). You can use any equivalent ratio as the starting point. How could you find the number of miles for a ½ hour from knowing 90 miles are driven in 2 hours? You could divide 2 hours by 4 to get a ½ hour, then divide 90 miles by 4 to get 22.5 miles. Sometimes it is easier to use a ratio other than the unit rate. This reasoning provides a focus on efficiency regarding *how* the ratios are manipulated to foster flexibility in thinking about ratio tables.

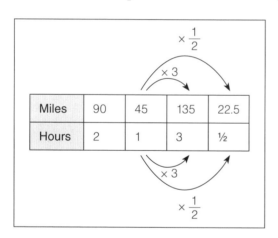

Figure 2.11: Completed ratio table.

When you multiply both quantities in a ratio by the same factor, you are using the relationship *between* equivalent ratios, knowing that multiplying both quantities by the same number will provide an equivalent ratio. Multiplying each part of the unit rate by the factor desired to obtain either 3 hours or a ½ hour produces the correct ratio. The ratio table is an effective way to simultaneously represent both *within* and *between* relationships.

How can you use the ratio table in other ways to demonstrate proportional relationships? What patterns do you see in the ratio table that help develop equivalent ratios? One advantage of using a ratio table is the ability to combine ratios to create new ratios. You may have seen this relationship in the table in figure 2.11. You can also combine entries in a ratio table together. For example, the task states that Lily drives 90 miles in 2 hours, and the ratio table shows that can also be expressed as 45 miles driven in 1 hour. You can determine an equivalent ratio by adding these ratios together to show that Lily could also drive 135 miles in 3 hours (see figure 2.11). You can combine additional ratios, or combinations of ratios, as well. Imagine that you want to determine how far Lily would drive in 8 hours. How could you determine the distance? You could multiply the unit rate of 45 miles for 1 hour by 8, you could multiply the given rate in the problem (90 miles in 2 hours) by 4, or you could add two 3-hour distances (135 miles plus 135 miles) and then add the 2-hour distance (90 miles). All of these methods provide the correct distance traveled of 360 miles.

Graph

How would you graph this relationship? Remember, you are thinking about 90 miles driven in 2 hours as well as other equivalent ratios. Which quantity would you represent on the *x*-axis and which on the *y*-axis? You should end up with a graph similar to the one in figure 2.12.

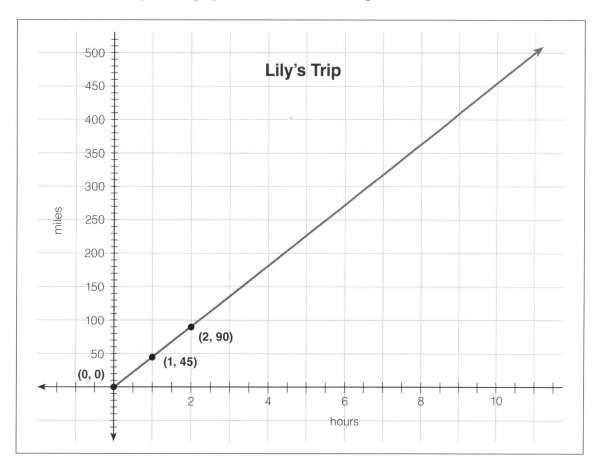

Figure 2.12: Graph representing the ratio of 90 miles in 2 hours.

Which value represents the independent variable, and which value represents the dependent variable? In other words, which quantity depends on the other? In considering the two different variables in this situation, time is independent of distance traveled, as time passes whether or not any driving occurs, but in order to drive any number of miles in a car, time must pass. Therefore, the number of miles is dependent on the number of hours that Lily drives. In the context of this problem, the number of hours is the independent variable and should be represented on the *x*-axis. The number of miles driven is the dependent variable and is represented on the *y*-axis. In this manner, you have connected proportional relationships, graphing, and the use of variables.

What are the characteristics of the graph that relate to representing proportional relationships? Note that the line starts at (0, 0). This is an important feature of graphs of proportional relationships and a way to think about them in connection with linear relationships, which are explored in chapters 3 and 4. A linear relationship may intersect the *y*-axis at any *y*-value; however, linear models of proportional relationships will include (0, 0) as a value. A proportional relationship can also be described as *direct variation* and is modeled using the equation $y = mx$—in this case, $y = 45x$, where *x* is the number of hours traveled and *y* is the number of miles. This equation diverges from ways that students represent multiplication in equations in the intermediate grades. Students in grades 3–5 write equations so that the number of groups is the first factor in the multiplication expression, meaning the equation would be represented as $y = x45$. This is in contrast with how equations are expressed when there are variables involved. It is common to place the coefficient before the variable, so that $y = 45x$. This difference should be discussed with students to minimize confusion regarding how relationships with variables are described. Also note that the line does not include negative values. This is specifically because the values for the number of hours driven can only be positive. Also notice that there is a line on the graph connecting the values that represent equivalent ratios in this task. Is connecting the points with a line appropriate in this context? It is appropriate, because both quantities (hours and miles) in the ratio are continuous and therefore all values of the independent variable—and dependent variable—are possible (as long as they are positive). What is a proportional relationship that would not be modeled with a line but only with points?

You should be mindful of whether or not it is appropriate to connect the points on graphs, as there are situations where it would not be appropriate to connect all of the points with a line. As with a double number line, situations where you would only have whole number increments, such as determining the number of buses for a field trip, should not be represented using a continuous line. However, unlike with the double number line, with a graph, there is a way to accommodate these sorts of data, by using discrete points.

Each of the representations explored allows you to communicate and analyze your thinking about the mathematical relationship of 90 miles in 2 hours. Furthermore, each representation lets you highlight various aspects of the relationship. For example, the bar model, double number line, and ratio table highlight the relationship between the unit rate and other equivalent ratios. The ratio table allows you to see how ratios can be multiplied by the same constant or added together to create equivalent ratios. Finally, the graph can represent an infinite number of equivalent ratios at the same time, as well as represent elements that are studied in chapter 4, such as slope (which is the unit rate of the situation). Each of these representations supports reasoning and sense making using ratios and proportional reasoning and helps represent and communicate mathematical thinking to solve problems. When *students* are given the opportunity to consider which representations to use and understand the benefits different representations offer in solving specific tasks rather than being directed by the teacher, the students are applying Mathematical Practice 5, "Use appropriate tools strategically," where the different representations are considered tools. This also provides an opportunity to consider the *layers of facilitation*. Students may need whole class facilitation to make sense of the models, how they can be used, and the benefits of each one. As students explore ratio tasks, facilitation can shift to small groups and ultimately to individual students. This facilitation can then shift to focus on flexibility in representations and using the models effectively to solve problems.

Exploring Varied Proportional Problem Types

In their research on middle-grades mathematics, Kathleen Cramer and Thomas Post (1993) identified three problem types that provide the foundation for proportional reasoning. The investigation of these types provides different ways to understand proportional reasoning. Before learning the names of the types of problems, consider the proportional reasoning tasks in figure 2.13. Each problem represents one of the three types. How are they the same? How are they different?

1. The scale on a map is "2 centimeters represents 25 miles." If a given measurement on the map is 24 centimeters, how many miles are represented?

2. Lauren and Kenneth purchased pencils. Lauren bought 10 pencils for $3.50, and Kenneth purchased 5 pencils for $1.80. Who got the better deal?

3. Kimberly is making paint to use in art class. Yesterday, she mixed white and red paint together. Today, she used more red paint and the same amount of white paint to make her mixture. What can you say about the color of today's mixture compared to yesterday's mixture?

Figure 2.13: Proportional reasoning tasks.

The first problem is a *missing-value problem*. Three of the four values of a proportion are provided in the problem, and you need to find the remaining—or missing—value. Many proportional reasoning problems are missing-value problems. This problem type requires you to consider the relationship of a given ratio and then determine an equivalent ratio.

The second problem is a *numerical-comparison problem*, where you are provided two ratios and you must determine a relationship between them (greater than, less than, or equal) to respond to the task.

The third proportional reasoning problem is a *qualitative-reasoning problem*. It asks you to reason without numbers, to think about tasks qualitatively. By attending to problems that emphasize qualitative reasoning, you can focus on the reasoning about the proportional relationship without having the numbers to distract you from the thinking. In the given problem about paint, three possible results can occur: the color can be the same, the color can be less red, or the color can be more red. The given information (more red paint in the second mixture and the same amount of white paint in both mixtures) helps you conclude that the color Kimberly mixed today is more red than yesterday's mixture.

Students should be provided opportunities to reason with each problem type and with many different contexts. Sense making is a key ingredient to solving ratio and proportional relationship problems. How you reason about problems and which solution pathway you choose should be influenced by the context of the problem.

Consider the first problem in figure 2.13. How would you reason about this problem based on the context? What representation would you choose, and why? Consider the double number line (see figure 2.14).

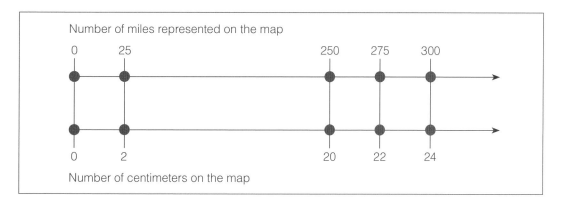

Figure 2.14: Double number line for scale on a map task.

In the double number line, you see the representation of the scale of the map as 2 centimeters (cm) is the same as 25 miles. The next step shown on the double number line is multiplying each quantity by 10, creating the equivalent ratio of 20 cm represents 250 miles. Adding the original ratio two more times shows you that 24 cm on the map represents 300 miles. One benefit of the double number line is that the representation actually feels like you are connecting to the measurement of distance.

You might also solve this problem without drawing a model. How might the unit rate be applied? By dividing 25 miles by 2 cm, you get the unit rate for this situation is 1 cm represents 12.5 miles. You can multiply the unit rate of 12.5 miles per cm by 24 cm to find out the total distance represented is 300 miles. No matter what strategy you use, the underlying ratio relationship provides equivalent quantitative comparisons between the scale distances on the map and the corresponding distances in the real world.

Now consider the second problem in figure 2.13 (page 55). How would you solve this problem? How would you organize the information to make sense of it? You could use division to find the unit rate that each person paid for the pencils. You would divide $3.50 by 10 and $1.80 by 5 to conclude that each of the pencils Lauren purchased cost $0.35 and each of the pencils Kenneth bought was $0.36 per pencil. Therefore, Lauren got the better deal.

A second method involves altering one relationship so that it includes a quantity present in the other relationship (such as having the same number of pencils or the same cost for each person). You could determine the amount Kenneth would need to pay for 10 pencils and use it to compare to Lauren's cost for 10 pencils. If Kenneth purchased 10 pencils at his cost, he would pay $3.60, which is more than Lauren paid for her 10 pencils. Why was the number of pencils compared instead of the cost for the pencils? In looking at the quantities of pencils (5 compared to 10) and the cost for the pencils ($1.80 and $3.50), it was more efficient to double the number of pencils that Kenneth bought so that they both would be purchasing the same number of pencils rather than to determine a common cost between $1.80 and $3.50. In both approaches, when you attend to the underlying proportional relationships, you come to the conclusion that Lauren made the better purchase.

Another way to determine who got the better deal is to use what some call the *butterfly method*, shown in figure 2.15.

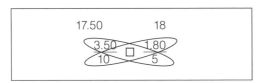

Figure 2.15: Butterfly method to compare ratios.

In this method, the first quantity of the first ratio is multiplied by the second quantity of the second ratio and vice versa. The products are assigned to the first quantities of the ratios. The greater product indicates the greater ratio. In figure 2.15, you see that 5 pencils for $1.80 is more expensive than 10 pencils for $3.50 because the ratio is connected to the greater product of 18 compared to 17.50. Although you can correctly compute the result as shown in figure 2.15, the mathematical meaning behind the calculation is often lost. Some simply follow the procedure without understanding. In problem solving that focuses on sense making, strategies and procedures without meaning are not helpful. As such, teaching this method is not recommended, especially when students are beginning to make sense of ratios and proportions. Following a method without understanding leads to misconceptions and a lack of application and connection among mathematical problems, concepts, and procedures. This discussion is continued later in this chapter in regard to this cross-products strategy.

Using Proportional Thinking With Percent

Another important use of proportional reasoning is the application to percent problems, such as the investment task in figure 2.16.

Heidi and Meredith decide to invest money in a local ice cream shop. Heidi invests $1,500, which is 60% of their total investment. How much do Heidi and Meredith invest together?

Figure 2.16: Ice cream shop investment task.

Which problem type is this task? How would you go about making sense of this problem? This task is a missing-value problem; you need to determine the missing total investment. Working with percentages is a way of using proportional reasoning; percent can be represented using ratios. A percent is a comparison out of 100, so this problem involves thinking about the ratio of Heidi's investment compared to the total investment, which is $^{1,500}/x$ and 60 percent, or $^{60}/_{100}$. You might choose to explore this task using a bar model (see figure 2.17).

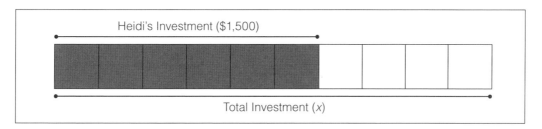

Heidi's Investment ($1,500)

Total Investment (x)

Figure 2.17: Bar model of the ice cream shop task.

In this representation, you can see that Heidi's investment is six parts of the whole, which can be thought of as comprising ten parts. This is a representation of 60 percent, which is six parts out of ten parts, the whole. You can see that each of the six parts of Heidi's investment is worth $250 by dividing her $1,500 investment by 6, and the entire investment is $2,500 because 10 × 250 = 2,500. How is this different from how you typically solve similar problems? How can you use this same type of reasoning to solve problems involving percent when different values are missing in the problem? For example, how could you use this to find out what percentage $1,500 is out of an investment of $2,500? What if you were looking for what 60 percent of the investment was if the total investment was $2,500?

Often with these sorts of problems, students are directed to use what is sometimes described as the "is over of equals percent over 100" strategy, or $^{is}/_{of} = {}^{\%}/_{100}$. In this strategy, students look for the key words *is* and *of* to determine what goes where in writing the proportion. In this case, the students are asking the question "$1,500 is 60 percent of what number?," so the *is* becomes $1,500 and the *of* becomes the unknown. When procedures like this are suggested too early, students lose the opportunity to make sense of the problem and engage in proportional reasoning; instead, they rely too heavily on key words. This can lead to unnecessary errors. For example, in the problem in figure 2.16, the *is* connects to the percent, not the part, so students may have difficulty following this procedure accurately. Procedures without understanding often lead to errors in solutions later as students solve problems like these on their own and rely on procedures instead of mathematical sense making.

Developing Proportional Reasoning Procedures

As students develop depth in their thinking about ratios, it is appropriate for them to begin to use more efficient procedures. It is important that conceptual understanding precedes this transition. Consider the situation presented in the fruit punch task in figure 2.18.

Angel is planning a party for 60 people. She decides to make a fruit punch that includes using 1½ pints of orange juice for every 8 servings. If she wants to prepare 1 serving for each person, how much orange juice will she need?

Figure 2.18: Fruit punch task.

How would you reason about the amount of orange juice she will need? How could you use a visual model to represent your thinking? Consider the double number line in figure 2.19.

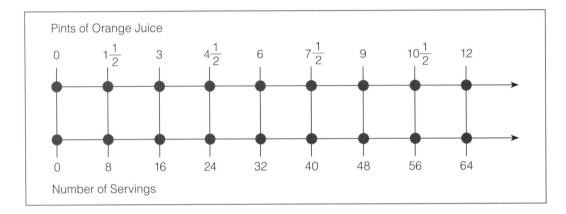

Figure 2.19: Double number line representation for fruit punch task.

This representation may help you see the relationship between the number of servings and the pints of orange juice needed for the fruit punch. How does the number of servings relate to the amount of orange juice needed? In other words, you might think about how many groups of 8 servings are needed for 60 people. From the double number line, you can see that the number of pints of orange juice needed is between 10 ½ pints (the number of pints needed for 56 people) and 12 pints (the number of pints needed for 64 people). Since 60 is halfway between 56 and 64, you know that you need halfway between 10 ½ and 12 pints of orange juice. That will tell you how many pints of orange juice (11¼) are needed for the fruit punch.

Another way to think about this task is to think about the number of groups of 8 people in 60 people. There are seven full sets of 8 in 60, with 4 left over. This means that there are 7 4/8 (or 7 ½) sets of 8 servings to get to 60 servings. Based on this reasoning, Angel needs 7 ½ groups of 1 ½ pints of orange juice.

There are other methods you can consider when solving this task; however, you should be cautious to not introduce less-transparent procedural methods too soon and thus take away from the development of conceptual understanding. When reasoning to solve tasks similar to this it is helpful to begin by using a tool or thinking about the number of groups to make sense of the problem and then you should transition to more efficient, numerical methods for determining the solution to the task. These numerical methods build on the sense making that has taken place in modeling the task using proportional reasoning. Look at the work shown in figure 2.20, which describes one way to determine the amount of orange juice Angel needs.

Although this process leads to the answer in a transparent way, it is not efficient. Now that you have developed a conceptual understanding of proportional relationships, it is appropriate to consider the *cross-products strategy*. To use the cross-products strategy for this task, you need to identify the two equivalent ratios in the problem. The first ratio is from the recipe for the fruit punch. Angel needs 1 ½ pints of orange juice for 8 servings of fruit punch. The second ratio is the amount of orange juice needed to create a fruit punch to serve 60 people. A proportion demonstrates that two ratios are equivalent. For this task, you could set up the proportion $^{1½}/_8 = {}^x/_{60}$ (note that you could also create the proportional relationship of $^{1½}/_x = {}^8/_{60}$). Multiply each initial quantity by the second quantity in the opposing ratio, which in this problem creates $(1½)(60) = 8x$. Solving for x determines that

> 7 ½ groups of 1 ½ pints
>
> is the same as
>
> (7 ½ groups of 1 pint) plus (7 ½ groups of ½ of a pint)
>
> is the same as
>
> (7 ½ pints) plus (7 groups of ½ of a pint) plus (½ of a group of ½ of a pint)
>
> is the same as
>
> (7 ½ pints) plus (3 ½ pints) plus (¼ of a pint)
>
> for a total of
>
> 11 ¼ pints of orange juice

Figure 2.20: Number of pints of orange juice.

x is equal to $^{90}/_8$, or 11 ¼. This is the same answer you determined in the earlier process. While this strategy provides a more efficient alternative to solving the task, it is important that this procedure is used in the context of making mathematical meaning. Many follow the steps with little attention to the proportional reasoning that is the foundation of the cross-products strategy. As a result, the use of the cross-products strategy often does not support the reasoning goal of a focus on ratio and proportional relationships and should only be incorporated into instruction once there is a firm understanding of the conceptual underpinnings related to proportional reasoning.

So why does this method work? What is really happening when you multiply 1 ½ by 60 and x by 8 in $^{1½}/_8 = {}^x/_{60}$? In the ratio of 1 ½ pints of orange juice to 8 servings of punch, how many pints of orange juice would be needed for 16 servings? Since 16 is double 8, you can double 1 ½ to get 3 pints. This new ratio would be 3 pints of orange juice to 16 servings. In this way, you have multiplied each part of the ratio by the same term (using the between relationship), in this case 2. What if you multiplied each part of the ratio by 60? What would the ratio become? You know that 60 times 1 ½ is 90 pints of orange juice. Likewise, 60 times 8 is 480 servings of punch, so this becomes a ratio of $^{90}/_{480}$. Follow a similar process to determine the other equivalent ratio. Starting with the ratio $^x/_{60}$, multiply both quantities by eight, and you get $^{8x}/_{480}$. Replacing each ratio from $^{1½}/_8 = {}^x/_{60}$ with these equivalent ratios, you get $^{90}/_{480} = {}^{8x}/_{480}$. Like in the pencil task, when one part of both ratios is the same, the other part can be compared. Since we have made the total number of servings both equal to 480, then the number of pints of orange juice in both ratios must also be the same. So $90 = 8x$, the same equation as the one using the cross-products strategy. The cross-products strategy is based on an understanding of equivalency with fractions or ratios.

Before the cross-products strategy is introduced, this understanding should be developed so that the procedure makes sense mathematically.

We developed topics in ratio and proportional relationships in this chapter with the goal of achieving conceptual understanding before the use of computational procedures. This will enhance the development of mathematical proficiency. Students need to reason with a wide range of rational number concepts and be able to use quantitative and qualitative comparisons and process multiple pieces of information simultaneously. These abilities support the kind of proportional reasoning mentioned at the beginning of this chapter. This type of thinking should lead to more efficient problem-solving strategies. For example, consider the following similar triangles task (in figure 2.21).

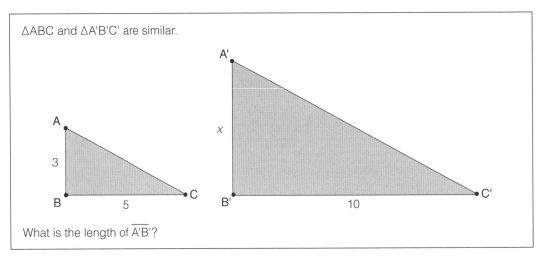

Figure 2.21: Similar triangles task.

A common way to solve problems like this is through the use of the cross-products strategy as in figure 2.22. The calculations are not difficult, but are they necessary?

There is another, more efficient strategy you could have used to determine the length of the missing side. You could multiply each of the side lengths of ΔABC by 2 to determine the lengths of the corresponding sides of ΔA'B'C'. Sense making means more than simply using the cross-products strategy to solve problems; it means applying reasoning strategies to solve each problem efficiently. This focus on reasoning is a byproduct of the initial focus on exploring ratio and proportion problems conceptually prior to procedurally as we described in this chapter.

$$\frac{AB}{BC} = \frac{A'B'}{B'C'}$$

$$\frac{3}{5} = \frac{x}{10}$$

$$3 \cdot 10 = 5 \cdot x$$

$$30 = 5x$$

$$\frac{30}{5} = \frac{5x}{5}$$

$$6 = x$$

Figure 2.22: Using the cross-products strategy to determine the length of the missing side of a triangle.

Identifying Proportional Relationships

While the examples provided in this chapter thus far represent proportional relationships, you also need to consider non-examples of proportional reasoning to ensure complete understanding. Consider the problems in figure 2.23.

1. Gloria drives at an average rate of 25 miles per hour for 3 hours to get to her friend's house. How long will it take her if she is able to average 50 miles per hour?

2. Judy's cell phone service charges her $14.50 per month for phone service, plus $0.15 for each text she sends or receives. Last month, she sent or received 27 texts and her bill was $18.55. How much will she pay if she sends or receives 54 texts this month?

3. Randy and Jorge both go for a run. When they run, both run at the same rate. Today, they started at different times. Randy had run 3 miles when Jorge had run 2 miles. How many miles had Jorge run when Randy had run 6 miles?

Figure 2.23: Nonproportional reasoning tasks.

In the first example, it will actually take Gloria one-half the amount of time if she travels at twice the speed. She will get to her friend's house in 1½ hours at a rate of 50 miles per hour. This situation is not proportional. When two quantities are proportional, they will always be in the same ratio. In the first example, 25 miles per hour for 3 hours is not the same ratio as 50 miles per hour in 1½ hours. As Gloria's average speed increases, the time it takes to complete the trip decreases. This situation is *inversely* proportional, as the change in one quantity is inversely related to the other quantity (as one doubles, the other is halved).

In the second example, the cell phone bill this month will be $22.60, which is not double the previous bill, even though Judy sent or received twice as many texts. Since there is an initial cost involved, the relationship is not proportional, but rather it is an example of a linear relationship (see chapter 3). For the quantities to be proportional, both quantities should be zero at the same time and when one quantity doubles (such as the number of texts), then the other quantity should double (such as the amount of the bill). Neither of these requirements is met in the second example.

In the last example, the relationship is actually additive, not multiplicative, as the two runners are running at the same rate. This means that Randy will always be one mile ahead of Jorge. It is important to include these types of examples while learning about proportional reasoning in order to be able to distinguish between situations that are proportional and those that are not.

What about when proportional reasoning is embedded within a problem? Consider how you use proportional reasoning in the task in figure 2.24. Take a moment to complete this task before you continue.

It takes Jeremiah 4 hours to build a model airplane. It takes Nathaniel 2 hours to build the same model airplane. How long would it take them if they were to build the model airplane together?

Figure 2.24: Building a model airplane task.

What is this problem asking? How might you solve this problem? One of the first things you may notice is that it takes Jeremiah twice as long as Nathaniel to finish the model. While this is true, it, alone, does not provide enough information to solve the problem directly. How can you use that information to help you reach a solution?

One way to think of this problem is to determine how much of the model each individual would complete in 1 hour. Using the information provided in the problem, Jeremiah would finish ¼ of the model in 1 hour and Nathaniel would finish ½ of the model in 1 hour. Finding the rate at which each person can complete the model is a key component to determining how much they could complete together in 1 hour.

How does this thinking help you determine the total amount of time that it would take both boys to finish the model if they are working together? During each hour, Jeremiah would complete ¼ of the model and Nathaniel would complete ½ or ²⁄₄ of the model. How much of the model would the boys complete if they work together? Knowing that ¼ + ²⁄₄ = ¾, Jeremiah and Nathaniel would complete ¾ of the model in an hour if they worked together. Is the task complete? Although knowing how much of the model airplane they build in 1 hour is important, the question in the task is not yet answered. What is the question you are trying to answer? How does this information help you solve the problem?

You know that after 1 hour, the pair has completed ¾ of the model airplane and there is still ¼ of the model left to complete. One way to think about the total time needed to complete the model is to determine how much time it would take the pair to complete the unfinished part of the model. Think about the fact that there is ¾ of the model completed. How can you represent the amount of the model that remains to be completed in terms of how much has already been done (see figure 2.25)?

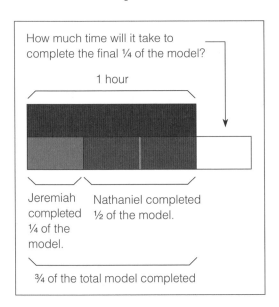

Figure 2.25: Visual representation of model airplane task.

Since ¼ of the model left to complete is the same as ⅓ of the ¾ of the model already completed, it would take the boys an additional ⅓ of the time it took to complete the ¾ of the model. Since it took 1 hour to complete ¾ of the model, the total amount of time it would take the boys to complete the model together is 1⅓ hours, or 1 hour and 20 minutes.

Another approach you might try would be to average the two lengths of time together, as the two people in the story are working together. You might think to add their times together and divide by two. Does that give you the correct answer? The answer in this case would tell you that it will take the boys three hours to build the airplane if they work together. However, since it takes Nathaniel only two hours to build the plane, it does not make sense for it to take longer if Jeremiah and Nathaniel work together. This is a misconception that sometimes occurs with this type of problem. Think about how you can appropriately model this problem using rates to avoid this misconception. To correctly model and solve the task in figure 2.24 (page 61), you must leverage your understanding of the mathematical connections among ratio, unit rate, fractions, equivalence, and addition. While there are several ways to solve this task, understanding unit rate, or the amount of the model each boy can complete in one hour, allows you to explore this concept through the lens of proportional reasoning and correctly solve this task.

The Classroom

Now that you have explored your own thinking about ratios and proportional relationships, it is time to explore what this could look like in the classroom. The following videos provide important insight into student thinking about the mathematics concepts addressed in this chapter. The first video underscores the foundational work needed in understanding percent by having students link percent to fractions and representing these number relationships with drawings. In this video, the students are asked to find the whole, given a part and the percent, when they explore the question "How many students are in class if 75 percent of the students are 24?" Watch the video prior to reading the rest of the chapter.

 www.solution-tree.com/Solving_a_Percent_Problem

Now that you have watched the video, what are your observations? What did you notice about the student interactions that are fostered by the teacher? How did the students reason with the task? How do the students connect percent relationships to fractions? Notice that many of the students draw a circle or bars to represent the entire class, and many of them split the whole into four parts, shading three of them. In answering the teacher's questions, students were able to explain their representations and how those representations connected to the task.

The teacher creates the expectation early on in the exploration that students make their mathematical thinking visible by asking them to draw models to represent their thinking. This verbally stated expectation is key in engaging the students in thinking about and discussing their understanding of percent. This also provides a means for the teacher to facilitate student-to-student dialogue and formatively assess what students are understanding and where there may be misconceptions. It is important to point out the significance the visual models play in this lesson because they provide the teacher and students with a connection between percentages and fractions. As with other ratio concepts, understanding percent with depth takes time. Although it would seem to be much more efficient for the teacher to provide students with a step-by-step procedure to determine how many students are in the class, doing so would limit the level of student engagement and understanding that results from that engagement.

What do you notice during the small-group interactions? What types of questions is the teacher asking? The small-group interactions in the video highlight how the teacher uses and references the student-created visual models as a way to foster students' mathematical understanding. Visual representations are not only important for the student who creates them; they are also vital to the other students in the class who interpret them. As such, it is essential that a teacher require students to make sense of other students' representations. The teacher's emphasis on students representing their thinking using visual models allows him to connect to the content goal of the lesson while addressing the mathematical needs of the students. This is accomplished by asking pointed questions while interacting with students. This focus on student thinking continues throughout the small-group and whole-class interactions in meaningful ways that support the advancement of student learning.

Another observation that you may have made is near the end of the video. The teacher asks the whole class how their drawings help them make sense of the problem. This question is used so that the students can synthesize what they learned during the lesson regarding how percent relationships relate to fractions and for the teacher to gather formative assessment data related to the understandings of the students in the class related to percent and fractions. Importantly, a student summarizes that he could see what the problem is asking by using a visual representation. The student's response underscores the importance of having students draw diagrams of the mathematical relationships in a problem, which is described in Mathematical Practice 1, "Make sense of problems and persevere in solving them."

The second video displays the various strategies students can use when analyzing proportional relationships to solve real-world and mathematical problems. In the video, you will observe a class of students who are exploring the following task (see figure 2.26).

You work in a grocery store. Your boss gives you the following table to make sure that the prices of various sizes of lemonade are proportional.

Fill in the missing values in order to determine the price or size of the lemonade.

Price ($)			1.50	3			9		16
Container Size (oz)	8	10		24	32	64		116	

Figure 2.26: Lemonade task.

Watch the video of students exploring the task prior to reading the rest of the chapter.

www.solution-tree.com/Using_a_Table_to_Reason
_Proportionally

Now that you have watched the video, ask yourself the following questions. How do the students connect the relationships of price to container size? Many of the students start with the given fact that the 24-ounce container has the price of $3. What strategies do they use to determine the other relationships?

Notice how the teacher leverages the students' mathematical intuitions to make sense of the situation provided in the problem and as a result engages the students in Mathematical Practice 2, "Reason abstractly and quantitatively." Throughout the lesson, the teacher encourages the students to make sense of quantities of cost and container size and the relationship between them. How does what the students say inform the actions of the teacher with the small groups? By carefully listening to what the students are saying as they work on the task in small groups, the teacher is able to learn about student thinking that leads to meaningful small-group and whole-class discussions.

How does the teacher prompt students to initially make sense of the task? After asking the students to investigate the task in small groups, he approaches various groups and asks them to describe their thinking about the problem. Each group demonstrates reasoning about the task in different ways, some of which are correct and some incorrect. How does the teacher use the formative assessment process to drive his questioning? Through assessment and questioning, the teacher is able to determine the understanding of various students and groups of students and to challenge their understandings with questions that advance their learning, including asking how they could justify the cost for an 8-ounce container of lemonade, supporting students making sense of unit rate. How does the teacher facilitate students discussing the problem within their groups? Notice how he engages students in Mathematical Practice 3, "Construct viable arguments and critique the reasoning of others," by helping students build on other students' reasoning.

At the end of the video, the teacher brings the whole class together to discuss the patterns they discovered in the table. Notice how the small-group conversations provide formative assessment data for the teacher to guide the whole-group discussion. Accordingly, he starts the whole-class wrap-up by discussing the price of an 8-ounce container of lemonade. The teacher's goal with this approach is to review the challenges that were apparent from determining the unit rate in small groups. The students are able to use both between and within relationships to determine the price of 8 ounces of lemonade as well as the cost for 72 ounces. Building on the conversations that took place during the small-group discussion, the teacher then asks the whole class if they can use the given relationship that it costs $3 to purchase 24 ounces of lemonade to determine what size lemonade container could be purchased for $9. This questioning advances student thinking beyond just using the unit rate. When students share their reasoning in the whole-group conversation, the teacher is able to address the thinking that surfaces during the small-group conversation and, in turn, is able to deepen the understanding of all of the students in the class.

TQE Process

At this point, it may be helpful to watch the first video again (page 63) and pay close attention to the tasks, questioning, and opportunities to collect evidence of student learning.

The TQE process can help you frame your observations. Teachers who have a deep understanding of the mathematics they teach:

- Select appropriate *tasks* to support identified learning goals
- Facilitate productive *questioning* during instruction to engage students in mathematical practices
- Collect and use student *evidence* in the formative assessment process during instruction

The *task* chosen provides a context for students to make sense of percent and connect percent concepts to fraction concepts. The wording of the task may not be optimal—"How many students are in class if 75 percent of the students are 24?"—which may cause some students to struggle. However, by specifically asking the students to draw a model, the teacher is providing an avenue for students to connect to the task and convey their thinking in meaningful ways. The models developed by the students provided insight into how different students were thinking about the problem as well as their prior knowledge of fraction models.

After watching the video with a lens toward the *questioning* that took place in the classroom, you probably noticed two factors that supported the students' engaging in Mathematical Practice 3, "Construct viable arguments and critique the reasoning of others." General questions like "What are you thinking about?" and "How can you explain your thinking?" initiated the expectation that the students verbalize their mathematical thinking. Whereas, more pointed questions like "What is he saying?" and "What does she mean by that?" obliged the students to make sense of another's thinking. As a result, the teacher shaped the classroom environment by establishing a shared responsibility of what constitutes productive talk with students.

How did the teacher collect *evidence* of student learning? Through the establishment of this shared responsibility for productive talk and questioning, the teacher is able to use the formative assessment process to provide evidence for what various students understand while also allowing the teacher and students to provide proper feedback to their classmates. For example, did you notice how the student reasons after the teacher asks how her classmate "used 24 in his picture"? Initially, the student states that her classmate "shaded in four squares in the circle and that represents 75 percent." Her response does not make sense, so the teacher is able to formatively assess what she understands (or does not understand) about the problem and is able to provide timely feedback to her by asking follow-up questions. At the point when the student cannot move her thinking forward, the teacher again brings in a tablemate to support the learning and help the entire group make sense of the justification for why there are thirty-two students in the class.

Now reflect on your own teaching. In what ways are you creating the expectations that students share their thinking? In what ways are you creating the expectations that students make sense of another's thinking? Although challenging, explore changes based on your answers to these questions. Remember that change takes time and patience, so you may consider emphasizing only one area to change at a time.

In the following section, you will review some of the common errors students make as they relate to ratio and proportionality. This will provide you with another lens as you explore ways to support learners in the middle grades, particularly with knowledge of ratio and proportion.

The Response

Some students have difficulty correctly interpreting proportional relationships. For example, recall the similar triangles task in figure 2.21 (page 60). Examine the student work in response to this task (see figure 2.27).

What do you know about this student's thinking? What does the student understand, and where are the gaps in his or her reasoning? The student sets up the proportion appropriately, but the reasoning to solve for the missing value is faulty. The student likely thought additively, and since 5 + 5 is 10, the solution would be to add 5 to the 3 to get 8. The student might be confusing the process of adding ratios together to get a new equivalent ratio with multiplying the parts of a ratio by the same number to get an equivalent ratio. This student may be struggling moving from absolute thinking to relative thinking. A response to this error might be to further explore the use of ratio tables. Students who make this error might also make a similar error in a ratio table, but with the ratio table, the error may be more transparent to identify and to ultimately resolve. The ratio table expresses many

$$\frac{AB}{BC} = \frac{A'B'}{B'C'}$$

$$\frac{3}{5} = \frac{x}{10}$$

$$5 + 5 = 10, \text{ so}$$

$$3 + 5 = x$$

$$8 = x$$

Figure 2.27: Student work to determine length of the missing side of a triangle.

different equivalent ratios that allow both you and the student to examine additive as well as multiplicative relationships in the same table. This error may also be related to tricks learned in prior grades that students misapply. When exploring equivalency with fractions, for example, many students will summarize the procedure as "whatever you do to the numerator, you do to the denominator." While this is true multiplicatively, it is not true additively and can be a source of confusion and overgeneralization.

Another error that students make involves looking for patterns that are not actually there. Reconsider the lemonade task in figure 2.26 (page 64). Students may incorrectly assume that each row of the table increases at a constant amount. For example, in the bottom row, some students may see 8 and 10 and then determine that the next number is 12 from the pattern of adding two each time. They might also see the $1.50 to $3 as double and assume all the values for the price are double the prior value. When students make these errors, what questions can you ask in order to support the students' critiquing their own reasoning? Students develop habits of examining the table horizontally only and looking for a pattern within each row, not considering the proportional relationship between the quantities represented in the table. They are no longer reasoning about the task; instead, they are trying to make sense of numbers devoid of context and without examining underlying structures and relationships present in the context. Using questions that prompt students to connect their responses based on their representations to the context is important. In this task, the table was intentionally designed so that there is not a consistent horizontal pattern. This intentionality supported the teacher's use of the formative assessment process in that he could see from the groups' answers if they were displaying this misconception.

It is helpful to anticipate the challenges students may face when exploring ratio and proportion concepts. Also, some students are able to use ratio and proportion procedures but are unable to justify these same procedures. One way to help students build a deep understanding is through the use of context and representations. Students should use representations and models of their thinking related to these contextual situations as ways to demonstrate their contextual understanding of proportional reasoning.

Reflections

1. What do you feel are the key points in this chapter?

2. What challenges might you face when implementing the key ideas from this chapter? How will you overcome them?

3. What are the important features for developing an understanding of proportional reasoning, and how will you ensure your instruction embeds the support needed for these features?

4. Select a recent lesson you have taught or observed focused on proportional reasoning. Relate this lesson to the TQE process.

5. What changes will you make to your planning and instruction based on what you read and considered from this chapter?

CHAPTER 3

Equations, Expressions, and Inequalities

In the elementary grades, students explore numbers and unknowns to make sense of operations; in the middle grades, students extend that work to include variables, where unknown values can be replaced by numbers to make equations true. Focus is placed on making sense of independent and dependent variables, equivalent expressions, and order of operations. Students find ways to describe sequences by using patterns. For example, when determining the nth term in a sequence, students begin by describing the first few terms in the sequence with the ultimate goal of finding a generalization to describe any term.

The Challenge

The initial task in this chapter (see figure 3.1) examines a series of staircases to generalize how many 1×1 squares are in any staircase. Before reading on, determine the number of 1×1 squares in a 5-step staircase and a 10-step staircase, and then determine a generalized expression for the number of 1×1 squares in an n-step staircase. Pay particular attention to how you developed your expression. Challenge yourself to either justify your expression in another way or to create a new expression that represents an n-step staircase.

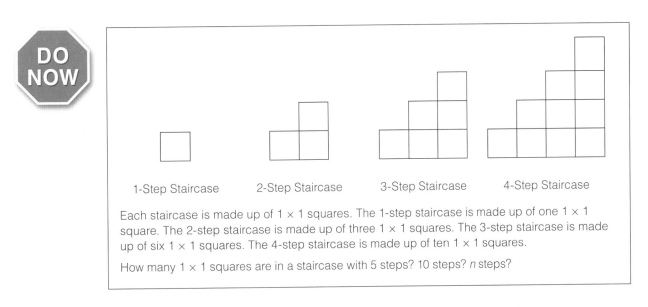

Each staircase is made up of 1×1 squares. The 1-step staircase is made up of one 1×1 square. The 2-step staircase is made up of three 1×1 squares. The 3-step staircase is made up of six 1×1 squares. The 4-step staircase is made up of ten 1×1 squares.

How many 1×1 squares are in a staircase with 5 steps? 10 steps? n steps?

Figure 3.1: Staircase task.

How did you determine the number of 1×1 squares in a 5-step staircase? What about the 10-step staircase? How did you represent your thinking—a drawing, a table, or something else? In what ways did you use patterns to help determine the number of steps? You might have made drawings and then recorded your findings in a table, resulting in something like what is provided in figure 3.2 (page 70).

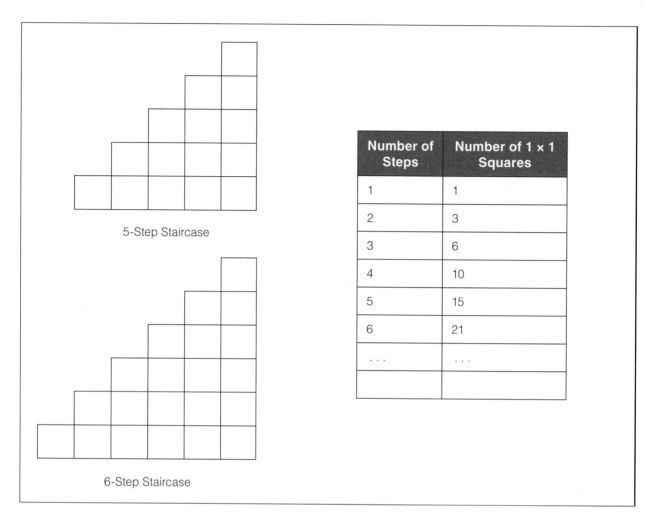

Figure 3.2: Drawing of 5-step and 6-step staircases with a table representation.

How can the patterns within the table help you determine a generalized expression for the number of 1 × 1 squares in any staircase? The values generated in the table can be described as a *sequence*, which is an ordered list of numbers, and each number in the sequence is called a *term*. This label of *term* can be confusing because term can also refer to a single number of the product or quotient of numbers or variables separated by addition or subtraction symbols in an expression. It is important to continually connect your use of the word *term* with the given context.

In this case, the terms in the sequence show that each subsequent staircase adds 1 × 1 squares equal to the step number of the staircase, so you might say the number of 1 × 1 squares in each staircase is the number of 1 × 1 squares in the prior staircase plus the current step number. In order to find the number of 1 × 1 squares in a 7-step staircase, you could take the number of 1 × 1 squares in the 6-step staircase and add 7. This type of thinking is known as *recursive thinking*. Although you will eventually arrive at the total number of 1 × 1 squares, a limitation with recursive thinking is that in order to determine the number of 1 × 1 squares in the *n*th step using recursive thinking, you would need to know the number of 1 × 1 squares in the staircase with *n* – 1 steps. For example, to find the number of 1 × 1 squares in a 10-step staircase using this recursive method, you would need to determine the number of 1 × 1 squares in every staircase leading up to that staircase (see figure 3.3).

Number of Steps	Number of 1 × 1 Squares
1	1
2	3
3	6
4	10
5	15
6	21
7	28
8	36
9	45
10	55

Figure 3.3: Determining the number of 1 × 1 squares using recursive reasoning.

Figure 3.3 shows that the number of 1 × 1 squares in the 10-step staircase is 55 squares. How does this help you determine the number of 1 × 1 squares in any staircase? A generalization allows you to find the number of 1 × 1 squares in any staircase. How can you determine an expression for the number of 1 × 1 squares? You could express the number of stairs for the first several staircases as sums of the stairs in the previous staircases. For example, the first staircase would be expressed as 1, the second would be 1 + 2, the third would be 1 + 2 + 3, and so on. Examine each expression with respect to how it connects to the pattern of staircases. This could lead you to the expression $1 + 2 + 3 + 4 + \ldots + n$. This expression connects back to the visual model provided in figures 3.1 and 3.2 (pages 69 and 70, respectively). If you observe each staircase and look at the columns of 1 × 1 squares, the first step in the staircase has one square, the second step has two squares, the third step has three squares, and so on. This can lead to a generalized formula in which you add all of the whole numbers from 1 up to and including the last step of the staircase. As you think about ways to generalize arithmetic, you also want to consider the efficiency of the different methods you develop. If you were asked to find the number of 1 × 1 squares in the 20th staircase using this formula, you would need to add $1 + 2 + 3 + 4 + \ldots + 18 + 19 + 20$. While there are multiple ways you could add these numbers together, it could become very cumbersome and prompts the exploration of more efficient methods to generate an expression.

As you think about finding generalizations, it becomes critical to begin to think in nonrecursive, explicit ways. *Explicit thinking* allows you to find any staircase in the sequence without relying on the previous term. Another way you might see the pattern is by adding on to each staircase so it becomes a square with the side length the same as the original base of the staircase (see figure 3.4, page 72).

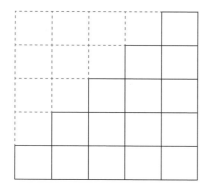

Figure 3.4: Adding on 1 × 1 squares to make the 5-step staircase a square.

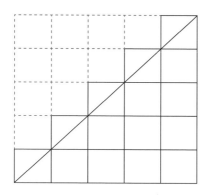

Figure 3.5: Dividing the square into two congruent triangles.

The length of the side of the resulting square is equal to the number of steps in the staircase, n, or in the case of the staircase in figure 3.4, the 5-step staircase leads to a 5 × 5 square. Now, the area of the resulting square is n^2, or 25 in the case of the staircase in figure 3.4. However, this large square is composed of more 1 × 1 squares than the original staircase. If you divide this large square into two congruent triangles by drawing the diagonal, the resulting picture looks like the illustration in figure 3.5.

The number of 1 × 1 squares below the diagonal is $n^2/2$, which for figure 3.5 is $25/2$ or 12 ½. You still have additional parts of the original staircase above the diagonal line. There are n 1 × 1 squares along the diagonal, so there are n half-squares above the diagonal, or $n/2$ squares, which, in this case, is $5/2$ or 2 ½. The total number of 1 × 1 squares in the staircase, then, would be $n^2/2 + n/2$ or 12 ½ + 2 ½ = 15.

Another consideration for a generalization is to re-examine the first expression, $1 + 2 + 3 + \ldots + n$. As stated previously, it is time consuming to add each of these numbers as n becomes larger. How could you use a pattern to help represent the generalization more efficiently by combining the terms of the expression (see figure 3.6)?

Consider the first term plus the last term in the expression. This equals $n + 1$. When you add the second term and the second-to-last term, you get $2 + (n - 1)$, or $n + 1$. This is true for all such pairs in the expression. As you continue to add these pairs, the next question to address is, How many pairs will you have? Since there are n terms in the sequence, you would have $n/2$ pairs. So, an expression for $n/2$ pairs of $(n + 1)$ is $(n/2)(n + 1) = n(n + 1)/2$.

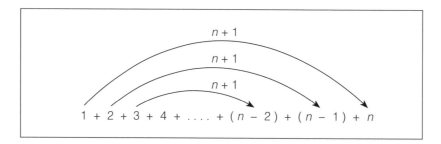

Figure 3.6: Pattern in arithmetic sequence.

With which Mathematical Practices were you engaged as you completed this task in finding the number of 1 × 1 squares in staircases of 5, 10, and n steps? It is likely that some of you were engaged in Mathematical Practice 1, "Make sense of problems and persevere in solving them." In determining a generalized expression for a staircase of 10 steps and then n steps, you probably made sense of the problem in multiple ways, including numerically and algebraically. As you examined other generalized forms of the expression, you were likely also engaging in Mathematical Practice 3, "Construct viable arguments and critique the reasoning of others." In making sense of different expressions, you examined arguments for why a particular expression would represent the given problem. Inherent in this task is also Mathematical Practice 7, "Look for and make use of structure." You examined a pattern and used the structure of connecting a pattern of geometric shapes made up of 1×1 squares to the pattern of adding numbers of an arithmetic sequence. The staircase task provides a way to explore structure to make sense of a geometric pattern and then to generalize that pattern as an expression. Within the generalized expression, structure is used to create the expression from both geometric shapes and number sequences and to compare them to each other.

As you engaged in examining different ways to define a generalization for the number of 1×1 squares in any staircase, you were also examining equivalent expressions. Properties such as the distributive property can be used to show that the expressions explored are equivalent. You can use fraction addition and the distributive property of multiplication over addition to determine that $n(n + 1)/2$ and $n^2/2 + n/2$ are equivalent expressions. By examining the ways these expressions connect to the context of the task, the equivalent expressions have meaning beyond abstract algebraic manipulation. This task is connected to a progression of mathematical concepts, which form the basis for exploring equations, expressions, and inequalities in grades 6–8.

The Progression

The development of understanding expressions, equations, and inequalities begins in the elementary grades with students making sense of patterns and word problems. As students write situation equations (see chapter 1 for a brief discussion of situation equations) for specific problems, they begin to develop the concepts underlying expressions, equations, and inequalities. We take the position that conceptual understanding must precede procedural fluency, and this applies to making sense of expressions, equations, and inequalities. Following is a progression within expressions, equations, and inequalities in grades 6–8.

- Explore equivalent expressions.
- Identify dependent and independent variables.
- Solve one-variable equations and inequalities.
- Solve real-world problems using numerical and algebraic methods.
- Connect proportional relationships, lines, and linear equations.
- Solve systems of two linear equations.

Writing expressions to match situations begins in kindergarten as students write situation expressions and equations to match word problems. For example, given the problem "Sarah has 5 stickers. Alex gives her 2 more stickers. How many stickers does Sarah have now?" students generate the equation $5 + 2 = \_\_\_\_$ to match the given situation. Students in grade 3 have developed the concept of unknown quantities and the ability to create equations to match situations involving all operations. Students in fourth grade generate and analyze patterns involving both shapes and numbers.

Grade 6

As students transition to the middle grades, they increase their formal use of algebraic expressions. Variables are used as a means of representing an unknown value. Instead of writing 8 + _____ = 11, students write $8 + n = 11$. Operations with whole numbers and fractions are extended to operations with variables that are used to stand for whole numbers and fractions. This transition is achieved initially by examining patterns and then abstracting these patterns to generalized expressions. Word problems become more complex, and algebraic expressions are used for making sense of the word problems. The parts of an expression are connected back to context. For example, if a student walks $4t$ miles in t hours, what is the meaning of the 4 in the problem? Problems that may have been previously solved numerically are now solved algebraically, helping students see connections between arithmetic and algebraic operations and supporting them as they move to more generalization in mathematics.

As students develop the concepts of generating algebraic expressions tied to contexts, they also begin to create one-variable equations and inequalities. Solving equations and inequalities is approached conceptually, and ideas of balancing across the equal sign, conserving inequalities, and using inverse operations become critical. For example, how can you find the original number if you know you multiplied that number by 4 and then added 3, with the result of 23? You could work backward with inverse operations. Since you added 3 last, you could subtract 3 first to undo that step. This tells you that after you multiplied by 4, you had the value 20. This means the original number was 5. The order of operations and use of grouping symbols continues to be important, as does the continued application of properties such as the distributive property, as students solve equations and inequalities in and out of context. Using tools such as the number line and the bar model helps provide connections between the visual and numeric representations of solutions. Additionally, the idea of equations having two variables is introduced through the discussion of dependent and independent variables and their connection to each other.

Grade 7

Algebraic expressions and equations continue to be a focus in grade 7. Real-world problems increase in complexity, requiring multiple steps to solve them. For example, you earn $4 per week for chores and have $12 already saved. You need $36 for a new video game. How many weeks will you have to save your money in order to purchase the video game? Equivalent expressions are examined using arithmetic properties including the associative property, the commutative property, and the distributive property all introduced in the elementary grades. The building of a generalized arithmetic and comparing equivalent expressions continue. As situations and patterns become more complex, there is an increased need to compare expressions. As students explore complex patterns and critique each other's reasoning, the use of properties is used to determine if one expression is equivalent to another. Application of equivalent expressions links to solving problems, and students recognize that solving one-variable equations can be thought of as a set of equivalent equations. Connections between numeric and algebraic expressions and equations continue to provide the foundation on which this increasingly complex understanding is built.

Grade 8

Expressions, equations, and inequalities are embedded in more complex situations and include integer exponents and radicals in grade 8. Systems of equations are explored through context-based problems to make sense of strategies and solution procedures. Additionally, proportional reasoning is connected to linear equations through similar triangles and slope. Slope is viewed as a rate of change and is connected to the concepts of ratio and proportion.

As students progress through the middle grades, their understandings of expressions, equations, and inequalities provide the foundation to make sense of functions beginning in grade 8 and progressing into high school concepts. High school mathematics draws on understandings of generalizing patterns with increasingly complex situations. Applications at the high school level include the use of multivariable situations and build on prior knowledge from middle-grades topics involving expressions, equations, and inequalities to reason about complex situations and make sense of higher-level mathematics.

The Mathematics

Much of the focus of the content of expressions, equations, and inequalities in the middle grades provides the groundwork for understanding algebra. As students make sense of real-world situations with unknown quantities that do and do not vary, they engage in algebraic reasoning. Students learn to write and solve expressions, equations, and inequalities, using context to help make sense of the language and structure of mathematics. Students in grades 6–8 must be able to write expressions and equations from context, solve equations and inequalities, investigate the concept of slope, and solve systems of equations.

Writing Expressions and Equations From Context

In language, an expression communicates an idea. The same can be said for algebraic expressions—they communicate what contexts represent. Interpreting context lays a foundation for making sense of algebra. Consider the task provided in figure 3.7.

You are cleaning out your desk at school. You find that you have 6 times as many pencils as highlighters. Write an equation for the number of pencils (p) in terms of the number of highlighters (h).

Figure 3.7: The pencils and highlighters task.

How did you set up your equation? When posed with this task, many people write the equation $6p = h$. How can you test this equation to see if it matches the context? When you start to substitute numbers for the variables in the equation $6p = h$, what do you notice? If you let p equal 12, then h is 72. Does this make sense in the context of the problem? Returning to the context, you realize that there should be more pencils than highlighters, in fact, six times more. Instead of thinking about the relationship between the number of pencils and the number of highlighters, the equation $6p = h$ was written to follow the order of the items presented in the task; whereas, the equation $6h = p$ correctly represents the mathematical relationship. This is an important example of the need to combine the language of mathematics—and possibly the use of the *key words* strategy—with sense making to ensure that the representation models the situation correctly.

With which Mathematical Practices were you engaged? Since the focus is on mathematizing the context of relating the number of pencils to the number of highlighters, you used Mathematical Practice 4, "Model with mathematics." Modeling with mathematics is an important aspect of work with expressions and equations in the middle grades. You were also engaged in Mathematical Practice 2, "Reason abstractly and quantitatively," as you examined the abstract equation and substituted a value for p to find h and then checked to see if the value of h as it related to p made sense in the context of the problem.

Students learn to use contexts to model with mathematics. This often occurs in ways that are different than how many teachers learned to make sense of these situations. Consider the bridge task provided in figure 3.8. How would you solve it?

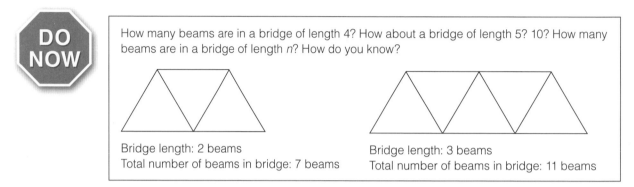

How many beams are in a bridge of length 4? How about a bridge of length 5? 10? How many beams are in a bridge of length n? How do you know?

Bridge length: 2 beams
Total number of beams in bridge: 7 beams

Bridge length: 3 beams
Total number of beams in bridge: 11 beams

Figure 3.8: Bridge task.

Often teachers reason in ways that mask a mathematical relationship. For example, you might make a table to solve this problem similar to the one provided in figure 3.9. How could you use this table to find the number of beams in a bridge of length n?

Bridge Length	Total Number of Beams
2	7
3	11
4	15
5	19

Figure 3.9: Table of values for bridge task.

The generalization, or the expression to find the bridge of any length, could be determined recursively by noticing the change from one term to the next. The number of beams increases by a constant rate of four beams from one bridge to the next. However, if you multiply the bridge length by 4 for each bridge, the number of beams is one too many for each bridge. This leads to the generalization of $4n - 1$ where n is the length of the bridge and the expression $4n - 1$ is used to determine the total number of beams.

This method for determining the generalization for the number of beams in a bridge of any length is fine; however, one limitation is that the total number of beams is tied exclusively to the use of the table representation. The meaning of the context is masked in the development of the expression. It may be difficult to connect each part of the expression back to the context. What if you reasoned visually instead? This may be challenging if you did not use the images of the bridge to determine a generalization. How *could* the visual of the bridge lead to a generalization? Consider the visual provided in figure 3.10.

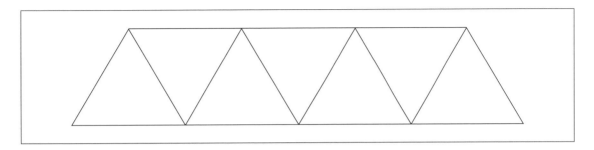

Figure 3.10: Visual for bridge task.

How can you generalize the pattern of the number of beams? How do you connect the visual with the generalization? Examine each of the generalizations provided in figure 3.11.

Each generalization is equivalent to $4n - 1$, but they were not determined using a table. Rather, each expression connects to a way of *visualizing* the bridge. How does the image of the bridge connect to each expression? In making sense of the expression $3 + 4(n - 1)$, where is the 3 in the visual? What about the 4? Why does the expression use $(n - 1)$ rather than n?

$3 + 4(n - 1)$

$n + 2n + (n - 1)$

$3n + (n - 1)$

Figure 3.11: Visualizing expressions for the bridge task.

Where does each term in the first expression connect to the visual in figure 3.10? The 3 can be seen in the first triangle. The 4 represents the number of beams added on to the bridge each time the length of the bridge increases by 1. The $(n - 1)$ can be more difficult to see. It represents the length of the bridge minus the first triangle. This is because the first triangle uses three beams, and each time the bridge length increases by 1 *after* the first triangle, 4 additional beams are added (see figure 3.12).

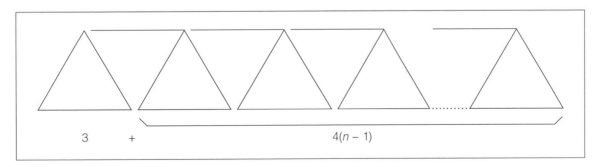

Figure 3.12: Visual for $3 + 4(n - 1)$.

Now that you have explored how an expression can connect to the visual image, revisit the second expression in figure 3.11. How does $n + 2n + (n - 1)$ connect to the visual in figure 3.10? To what part of the picture does the n connect? What about the $2n$ and the $(n - 1)$?

The *n* refers to the number of beams in the length of the bridge, or in the visual, the number of beams along the base of the bridge. The 2*n* refers to the beams that connect to the base of the bridge. The number of beams across the top of the bridge is 1 fewer than the number of beams along the base; therefore, that number can be modeled by the term *n* – 1.

How about the expression 3*n* + (*n* – 1)? This expression is probably easier to *see* in the visual in figure 3.10 (page 77) because of your work with the previous two expressions. The more you explore using a variety of representations to mathematize situations, the better you get at their use. The same is true for your students. In this expression, the 3 refers to the number of beams in one triangle; it is multiplied by *n* to indicate that the triangles are those that have a side that makes up part of the base of the bridge (see figure 3.13).

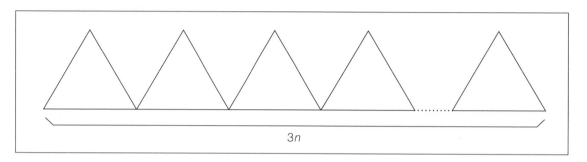

Figure 3.13: Visual for 3*n*.

The last term in the expression, (*n* – 1), describes the number of beams that connect the triangles at the top of the bridge. As in the previous expression, this makes sense because the number of beams at the top of the bridge is 1 fewer than the number at the base.

As in the pencils and highlighters task in figure 3.7 (page 75), the context of the problem is valuable in making sense of the expression. When students model with mathematics, it is important for them to refer back to the situation to make sure that their models are appropriate. However, sometimes the situation can lead directly to the generalization. In the bridges task, the expression was implicit in the visual model and it was not necessary to create a table to determine the generalization. When you are too quick to go to a procedure, like the process of making a table, you might miss an opportunity to *see* the mathematics in a more efficient way. Students may not always see a problem in the same way as either you or other students. Be sure to provide opportunities for them to share their thinking and make sense of the thinking of others. In doing so, you are supporting students to engage in Mathematical Practice 3, "Construct viable arguments and critique the reasoning of others." Encouraging students to make sense of problems on their own should also take place when solving equations and inequalities.

Solving Equations and Inequalities

Algebraic equations and inequalities allow you to represent and make sense of relationships between numbers. Consider the task in figure 3.14.

How did you make your decisions? Perhaps you tried substituting different numbers for *y*, or maybe you were able to reason without using substitutions. What type of justifications did you use for each comparison? Working with tasks like these helps you think about the number relationships that are represented in equations.

Which is greater in each equation, *x* or *y*? Is it possible for *x* and *y* to be equal? How do you know?

1. $x = -2y$

2. $x = \dfrac{y}{2}$

3. $x = y + 2$

4. $x = y - 2$

Figure 3.14: Comparing quantities task.

How did you make sense of the first equation? It might be easy to think that when you multiply a number by –2, the product will be less than the value with which you started, but what if *y* is a negative number? This is an important consideration in moving to more abstract ways of thinking and integrating new types of numbers into your relational thinking. How could you limit the types of numbers so that one variable will always be greater than the other? For example, if you only consider positive numbers for *x*, then the value of *x* will be greater than the value of *y*, as *y* would have to be negative to make the equation true. Or, if you only consider negative numbers for *x*, then *y* will be greater. If *x* is zero, then *x* and *y* are the same value. Therefore, for the first equation, *x* is sometimes greater than *y* and vice versa.

What about the second equation? Is *x* greater than *y*, or is *y* greater than *x*? Students will often confuse which is greater in this relationship. Again, in working with positive numbers, this may appear to be easy, as dividing a quantity by 2 will always be less than the whole quantity, making *y* greater than *x*. How do negative numbers affect this relationship? Is –1 greater than –½? This is one way to connect equations to a deep understanding of negative numbers, and again you see that sometimes *x* is greater, sometimes *y* is greater, and sometimes they are the same (again at zero).

How is the third equation different? Since this relationship is additive, the value of *x* is always two greater than the value of *y*. The same is true for the subtraction equation, where the value of *y* will always be greater than the value of *x*. In the primary grades, prior to the introduction to operations with fractions, students develop a certain understanding about the relationships of number and operation. In the intermediate grades, as students begin to multiply and divide with fractions, their understandings may need to be adjusted. Now, in the middle grades, students need to continue to examine equations and inequalities in light of the expansion of number systems to include negative numbers.

How can context be used to make sense of creating and solving an equation? Consider the task in figure 3.15.

Solve this problem using manipulatives. Also create an equation for the word problem and use the equation to solve the problem. Compare and contrast the methods.

Raspberries cost $4 more per pound than cherries. Abby pays $26 for 2 pounds of raspberries and 4 pounds of cherries. What is the price of a pound of raspberries? What is the price of a pound of cherries?

Figure 3.15: Word problem task.

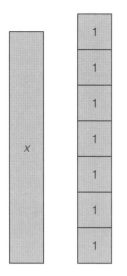

Figure 3.16: Representation of algebra tiles.

How could you express this situation using manipulatives? How could you represent an unknown quantity with a manipulative? It is likely that students have experience using base ten blocks, where the blocks are proportionate in size—1 ten is ten times larger than 1 one, 1 hundred is ten times larger than 1 ten, and so on. When a quantity is unknown, how do you determine what size to make the block? You can use algebra tiles to represent expressions with unknown quantities. Algebra tiles are designed so that the area of the tile that represents the unknown is purposefully not a multiple of the area of the tile that represents 1, as shown in figure 3.16. This is done to represent that the x tile is an unknown quantity.

Note that the x tile is not an integral multiple of the 1 tile—it appears to be between six and seven lengths of the 1 tile.

In the problem from figure 3.15 (page 79), if the variable, x, is the price per pound of raspberries, then the price per pound of cherries is $x - 4$. The equation would then become $2x + 4(x - 4) = 26$ to represent how much she spent on 2 pounds of raspberries and 4 pounds of cherries. Figure 3.17 provides a representation for the left side of this equation, or the expression $2x + 4(x - 4)$, using algebra tiles, first organized according to the terms in the expression and then organized so that like tiles are grouped by type.

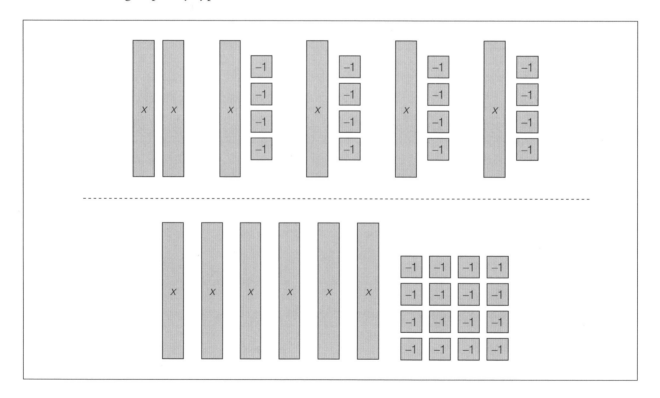

Figure 3.17: Manipulative representations of $2x + 4(x - 4)$.

How can you connect the algebra tiles in figure 3.17 to the symbolic representation? Examine figure 3.18.

As you can see, both the manipulatives and the symbols show that you can represent the left side of the equation to solve this task as $6x - 16$, by combining groups of the same type together with manipulatives, and by using expansion, the associative property of addition, and combining like terms with symbols.

$$2x + 4(x - 4) = x + x + (x - 4) + (x - 4) + (x - 4) + (x - 4)$$
$$= x + x + x + x + x + x - 4 - 4 - 4 - 4$$
$$= 6x - 16$$

Figure 3.18: Symbolic representation of $2x + 4(x - 4)$.

You know that you can express your equation as the equivalent equation of $6x - 16 = 26$. But what does this mean? Again, work to *make sense* of the problem. Think of this equation as a balance, where each side of the equal sign is the same value throughout the solution process (see figure 3.19).

The equation says that 16 less than $6x$ is 26. This means that $6x$ should be 16 more than 26, or 42. In thinking of the balance, that means that you can add 16 to both sides of the equation, maintain the balance, and still have the same value for x. This gives $6x = 42$. If you have six equal groups that total 42, there are seven in each group. This could be accomplished symbolically by dividing both sides of the equation by 6. Connecting sense making to the solution process for equations will aid students in understanding the equation-solving process. How does this process compare to how you typically solve similar

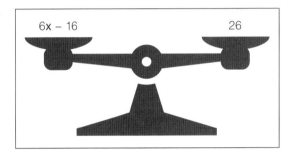

Figure 3.19: Balance representation of $6x - 16 = 26$.

problems and how you teach this topic to your students? Be careful to not apply inverse operations to solve equations before allowing students to make sense of the process and link back to the context first.

What if you thought of the price of raspberries in terms of the price of cherries as opposed to what was shared previously? How would the equation and subsequent reasoning used to solve the equation differ? Initially, the variable x represented the price per pound of raspberries. If x represented the price per pound of cherries, you could have the equation $2(x + 4) + 4x = 26$. How can both represent the same context? The key to understanding how both of the previous expressions can represent the situation is to consider how variables might be defined. In the first case, x represents the cost of one pound of raspberries; in the second, x represents the cost of one pound of cherries. You may feel that it makes more sense to set up the equation to look for the cost of one pound of raspberries, but the second equation is also a correct way to write an equation for this context. This is an important aspect of working with students. As stated previously, students may not always interpret a problem in the same way as either you or other students. Students need to be given the opportunity to make sense of the problem themselves before seeing how you thought about it.

Regardless of how the problem is presented and solved, you have to look back and determine what your mathematical answer means in the context of the problem and whether you have answered the questions provided in the task. When x is defined as the price per pound of raspberries, the solution to the equation $2x + 4(x - 4) = 26$ is $x = 7$. Therefore, in the context of the problem, the cost of one pound of raspberries is $7, and the cost of one pound of cherries is $3. Students tend to make errors when they fail to check that they are answering all that is asked in the problem. In this problem, you need to include the cost of one pound of raspberries *and* the cost of one pound of cherries.

Sometimes, you need to consider how the order of the information in the problem might have an effect on the solution. Take, for example, the application of percent in the task in figure 3.20. Make sense of the situation and then determine whose reasoning is correct.

The Dress Store is having a sale—30% off the price of all dresses. They have also distributed coupons that allow customers an additional 20% off the price of a dress.

- Riley is a clerk at the Dress Store. She says that the better deal comes from taking the 30% off from the price of the dress first, then the 20% off coupon.

- Paige is a customer at the store. She says that it works out better to take the 20% off coupon first, then the 30% off from the sale.

Who is correct, Riley or Paige? Explain your reasoning.

Figure 3.20: Multiple discounts task.

How did you answer which process is correct, since there is no price for the dress? One way is to select a price for the dress and determine what would be the result for each sequence. For example, if the original price of a dress is $100, then a 30 percent discount would be $30 off, which results in a new price of $70. A 20 percent off coupon would take an additional $14 off that price for a resulting final price of $56. For the other sequence, 20 percent off of $100 is $20, to give a price of $80. The next discount of 30 percent would be an additional $24 off the price, with the resulting price of $56—the same price as the first sequence. This would mean that the price would be the same whether you used Riley's method or Paige's method.

But at this point, you only know that the discount is the same for one dress price. How could you determine an answer regardless of the price of the dress? This is where you can use the benefit of the generalizability of expressions and equations. You could let a variable, say x, represent the original price of the dress and another variable, y, represent the final price of the dress. Using your understanding of percent and expressions, you can show a 30 percent discount as $x - 0.30x$. By combining terms with the same variable, $x - 0.30x$ is the same as $0.70x$. In other words, a 30 percent discount is equivalent to paying 70 percent of the price of the dress. In examining the two sequences, the first sequence (Riley's) is $y = (0.80)(0.70x)$. The second sequence (Paige's) is $y = (0.70)(0.80x)$. By using the commutative property of multiplication, you can demonstrate these two equations are equivalent. This means that no matter what the original price of the dress or the order in which the discounts are applied, the final price will be the same in each scenario. The cost is the same whether you use Riley's or Paige's method. As a result, both processes are correct. This task demonstrates how you can benefit from using the generalized form of expressions in solving problems.

Investigating the Concept of Slope

An important distinction between work in the intermediate grades and the middle grades is the progression from solving one-variable equations to relating two variables, one variable that is independent and another variable that depends on the first. Consider the definitions of *dependent* and *independent*. Dependent means relying on someone or something. Independent means not relying on someone or something. In science, plants need sunlight to grow. However, sunlight exists whether there are plants or not. The more sunlight, the more the plant grows (within reason). Therefore, the independent variable (sunlight) determines the value of the dependent variable (plant growth).

Reconsider the percent task presented in figure 3.20, where the equation could be written as $y = (0.70)(0.80x)$. Which variable is the independent variable, and which variable is the dependent variable? In this example, the original price of the dress (x) is the independent variable. The discounted price of the dress (y) depends on the original price of the dress, so it is the dependent variable. To graph this relationship on a coordinate plane, the independent variable is represented on the horizontal axis (often represented as x) and the dependent variable (often represented as y) is on the vertical axis.

Points on the coordinate plane are defined by both the independent variable and its associated dependent variable. For this context, a dress of $100 would cost $56 and would be represented by (100, 56) on the coordinate grid (see figure 3.21).

Figure 3.21: Graph of $y = 0.70(0.80x)$.

The graph is a linear relationship as well as a linear function (see chapter 4 for more information on functions). In the context of the problem, the graph should also only appear in the first quadrant. This is because all of the dress prices will be positive values. For the purpose of this discussion, the context will be represented by a continuous line to examine the mathematical relationship between the two variables. Also, two additional price combinations, one when a dress that originally cost $20 is discounted to $11.20, or (20, 11.2), and another when a $40 dress is discounted to $22.40, or (40, 22.4), are added to the graph (see figure 3.22, page 84).

Figure 3.22: Graph of *y* = (0.70)(0.80*x*) with connected points.

What is the point at which this line intersects with the *y*-axis? What does this mean in the context of the problem? For this graph, the *y*-intercept, the point where the line intersects the *y*-axis, is (0, 0). This is the amount of money you would pay, $0, if the dress originally cost $0.

How would you describe the relationship between the independent variable (the original cost of the dress) and the dependent variable (the discounted price of the dress)? One way is to relate how these two variables change in regard to one another. In this case, as the original price of the dress increases by $1, the discounted price of the dress increases by $0.56, so the rate of change is an increase of $0.56 per dollar (see chapter 2 for more regarding ratios and rates). This rate of change of the dependent variable, *y*, with respect to the independent variable, *x*, is commonly called the slope. In the graphical representation in figure 3.22, this is represented by the steepness of the line. As you move from one value of *x* to the next, the value of *y* changes by 0.56 times the change in the value of the *x* variable. Why is the steepness of the line valuable in your thinking about this problem? The steepness of this line corresponds to the increase in the discounted price compared to the increase in the original cost of the dress. If the discount was a different percentage, the steepness of the line would change. The slope of the line can be seen as a ratio of the change in the dependent variable to the corresponding change in the independent variable.

What Mathematical Practices does this investigation support? It supports Mathematical Practice 1, "Make sense of problems and persevere in solving them." In examining the discount situation, concepts of expressions and equations as well as slope begin to make sense. Additionally, the concept of slope is connected back to the context given, thus supporting Mathematical Practice 4, "Model with mathematics." As you make sense of the slope of the line, you are using the context to support understanding. The context led to making sense of equations and expressions, and the graphical representations linked back to the context in making sense of the meaning of slope.

Solving Systems of Equations

Eventually, situations are presented that need to be represented using multiple equations. Consider an extension to the previous multiple discounts task (see figure 3.23).

The Dress Store offers a special deal to its customers who join the Dress Store Club. When a customer joins the Dress Store Club, instead of the original 20% off coupon, they receive a coupon for 30% off the price of a dress, but the customer must also pay a fee of $10 per dress.

How can this new situation be represented? When is it better to use the Dress Store Club to buy a dress?

Figure 3.23: Extension to the multiple discounts task.

How did you represent this situation? You may have chosen an equation to represent the price of a dress using the dress club discount, which can be represented as $y = 0.70(0.70x) + 10$. How could you determine when the Dress Store Club is a good deal? One way to explore this scenario is to look at the graph of these two situations (see figure 3.24).

Figure 3.24: Two situations for multiple discounts task.

What do you notice about the graph? In considering how the line for the Dress Store Club prices is different than the first line you graphed, you should notice that the second line begins at the y-intercept of (0, 10), corresponding to the $10 Dress Store Club fee. If the original price of a dress is $0, you would still pay the $10 fee. The original discount graphed line begins at (0, 0).

You should notice that the original discount line is steeper than the Dress Store Club line. What do the slopes represent in this context? For both lines, the slope represents the amount of change in the discounted price compared to the amount of change in the original price. The important connection here is to the rate of change of each line. What is the difference in the rate of change in the two situations? For the first example, the rate of change is based on the 20 percent off coupon and the 30 percent off sale, or paying 80 percent of the original price and then 70 percent of that price, which was represented in the equation as (0.70)(0.80), or a rate of change of 0.56. For the second example, the rate of change is based on the 30 percent off coupon and the 30 percent off sale, which can be represented as (0.70)(0.70x), or a rate of change of 0.49. The differences in the coupons determine differences in the rates of change of the lines. In this case, the equation graphed is the price paid rather than the discount. The discount is used to determine the price paid, so the rate of change is the percentage of the original cost of the dress that was actually paid. The greater the percent off, the less the discounted dress costs and the less steep the line.

How do the differences in the y-intercepts and slopes impact these two situations? Since the second situation has a larger value for the y-intercept and a smaller positive value for the slope, the two lines intersect in the first quadrant. You can see this in the graph. Where do the lines intersect, and what does this mean for this situation? From the graph, the intersection occurs around the original dress price of $140. Dress prices under this original price are less expensive without the Dress Store Club; when dresses are greater than this original price, however, dress prices with the Dress Store Club are less expensive. At the point of intersection, the price paid is the same regardless of whether you use the Dress Store Club or not. This helps determine the exact value of the original dress price. The specific value can be determined by setting the original scenario, $y = (0.70)(0.80x)$, and the new scenario, $y = 0.70(0.70x) + 10$, equal to each other, which yields $142.86 (rounded to two decimal places) as the original price of the dress at which the discounted prices are the same.

Examining a system of equations such as this brings together many of the concepts of middle-grades algebraic reasoning—identifying and using dependent and independent variables, working with expressions and equations, using the characteristics of equations and graphs, and making sense of problems in context. Student understanding of systems of equations begins in the middle grades and is expanded in further development in high school mathematics courses. This extension is discussed in *Making Sense of Mathematics for Teaching High School* (Nolan, Dixon, Safi, & Haciomeroglu, 2016).

The Classroom

To this point, you have examined your own thinking about expressions, equations, and inequalities. Now, turn your attention to what this will look like in the classroom. The following two videos provide valuable insight into how students reason with expressions and equations and make sense of these mathematical concepts. The first video examines the bridge task (see figure 3.8, page 76), asking the students to determine how many beams are in bridges of varying lengths. This provides an exploration of how students can engage in problem solving and making sense of the mathematics involved in this problem. You are encouraged to watch the video in its entirety before proceeding.

www.solution-tree.com/Making_Sense_of_Models

Now that you have had an opportunity to watch students engaged in determining a generalized expression for the number of beams in the bridge, what are your thoughts? What did you notice about how the students engage with the task? What is the teacher's role? What types of questions does the teacher ask individuals, groups of students, and the whole class?

In this instance, the task provided is to determine the number of beams in bridges of length 5 and length 10. Perhaps you noticed the varied ways students work to determine this solution. Some draw pictures, while others build bridges with toothpicks. Notice as the teacher interacts with a small group of students, one student chooses to make a table of values and predicts that the number of beams will increase by four each time. This is verified by other members of her group who draw pictures or model with toothpicks to determine whether her prediction is accurate. The values in her table match their modeling of the situation. The students do not, however, work at this point to determine why her prediction may be correct. In the final element of the task, finding a generalized expression for any length bridge, students continue to engage in the task to determine how to find an expression. Tables and drawings are used to help justify expressions and to make sense of different representations.

In this video, the teacher chooses to engage students in Mathematical Practice 5, "Use appropriate tools strategically," and Mathematical Practice 4, "Model with mathematics." Students are given different tools to choose from, and they are also given the freedom to use the tools that make sense to them. What tools do the students use in this case? Toothpicks, drawings, and tables are all used by students to make sense of the problem and to help each other model the problem accurately. You may have noticed that even within one group, students use different tools to support constructing an expression to match the context. The task provides a way for students to model their mathematical thinking with a context of beams in bridges and to connect the mathematical expression to the context provided.

Consider the end of the video. The teacher uses the *layers of facilitation* to support student thinking. Based on facilitating small groups, the teacher provides an expression she says she saw a group determine, namely $4(n - 1) + 3$. The students are asked if this is a valid expression for the context, and, in making sense of it, the students connect back to the situation and how the bridges are created. Another group provides the expression $4n - 1$, and the teacher asks what the 4 in the expression represents. This brings the context back into play to make sense of why the expression works and how it connects to the situation.

In the next video, you will examine a task that asks students to make sense of equations of lines and their respective graphs, particularly determining when lines are parallel or intersecting. Take a moment to watch the video in its entirety before proceeding.

www.solution-tree.com/Exploring_Different_Ways_That
_Lines_Can_Intersect

In this video, students are asked to first predict which pairs of lines will be parallel and which will be intersecting. Notice that the task posed has multiple pairs of lines that will satisfy each conclusion. Students are asked to justify why they think lines are intersecting or parallel from the equations and then compare those to graphs of pairs of the same lines. What conclusions are students able to make? Rate of change is connected to the equations and the graphs to make sense of the mathematics involved. Students conclude that when slopes are equal, the lines can be parallel or the same line, and when slopes are different, the lines intersect.

In this case, students are engaged in Mathematical Practice 7, "Look for and make use of structure." The equations of the lines provide a mathematical structure to make sense of how two lines are the same or different. Examining the slope and y-intercepts of each line provides a connection to the structure of the graphical representations, and conclusions are made based on this structure.

TQE Process

At this point, it may be helpful to watch the first video (page 87) again and pay close attention to the tasks, questioning, and opportunities to collect evidence of student learning. The TQE process can help you frame your observations. Teachers who have a deep understanding of the mathematics they teach:

- Select appropriate *tasks* to support identified learning goals

- Facilitate productive *questioning* during instruction to engage students in Mathematical Practices

- Collect and use student *evidence* in the formative assessment process during instruction

The lesson's *task* in this case provides the opportunity for students to use a visual picture to make sense of generalizing an algebraic expression. The task first presents a numerical representation of the sequence of bridges, and the focus quickly shifts to determining an expression for the number of beams in a bridge of any length. By providing tools for students to use and a rich task with which to engage, the teacher fosters the learning goal in a meaningful way and students are able to make sense of the problem at hand. Additionally, the teacher is aware of multiple expressions to represent the beams in the bridge, providing her with the knowledge needed to support student reasoning throughout the layers of facilitation. The teacher's knowledge of these expressions is vitally important, as she must be aware of different ways to write expressions and to connect those expressions to the context provided to foster student sense making both of their own solutions and their classmate's solutions through facilitation of both small-group and individual learning.

The teacher uses *questioning* through small- and large-group interactions to promote learning. The teacher is deliberate in her questions and is intentional in fostering productive talk. Perhaps one of the first instructional moves that caught your attention is when the teacher says, "So I see you have a table; talk to me about it," recognizing that the students had already been talking in their group about it. A student proceeds to explain her table and why she made it. The student describes her prediction, and the teacher then checks with another member of the group who used toothpicks to model the relationship, asking if he was able to check the prediction provided in the table. The teacher is not making a judgment about rightness or wrongness of the table and the prediction; instead, she is helping to engage the group members in supporting each other and the productive discourse of the group. Since the other group members are able to verify the table, the teacher then prompts them by asking. "How can you find a bridge of length 10 without having to write the whole table to get to 10?" This prompts a third student in the group to provide a potential method for the bridge of length 10. After this student concludes the bridge of length 10 would have 35 beams, the teacher asks the other members of the group if they agree. They do not all agree and are then prompted to discuss and come to a consensus for their group. These teacher questions help support Mathematical Practice 3, "Construct viable arguments and critique the reasoning of others." As the video continues, you see the students continue to critique each other's solutions and solution processes with productive talk. The questions posed by the teacher provide thinking points for the students. Questions like "How could you do that without a table?" provide impetus for students to think differently and expand their understanding. Notice that the teacher is quick to ask students to explain their thinking and rarely confirms the correctness or incorrectness of an answer.

The students provide *evidence* of their learning as they participate in the conversation. As the teacher circulates among the groups, she notices that the students are in deep conversation about the task, and they have come to consistent conclusions that there are 39 beams in a bridge of length 10. This evidence provides the teacher with the knowledge that the class is now ready to move to a generalized expression. Here she is using the formative assessment process to guide her decision of when students are ready for the next part of the lesson. This does not require a tremendous amount of whole-class discussion, however. The teacher knows that the students understand methods of finding the number of beams in a bridge of length 10, and it is sufficient for the students to confirm their answer is correct. This then leads to the goal of the lesson, creating a generalized expression for the task.

Again, as the teacher facilitates small groups of students, she uses the formative assessment process to help determine where the students may need support and what questions are needed. Notice after giving the task to find an expression for a bridge of length n, she facilitates one group to support their use of a table to generalize the expression. Formative assessment helps her know how students are using a table and that they are struggling to determine an expression from their work. While it would have been easy for the teacher to give an answer, instead, she prompts them to think about the table in different ways and compare the values they need with the values they have in their table. She facilitates small-group interactions by providing the group with the scaffolding they need but still maintains the focus on student learning.

Finally, the formative assessment process, as well as teacher knowledge of various solutions to this problem, provides the avenue for the final examination of different expressions for the length of the bridge. Students are prompted to make sense of another group's work in a way that is meaningful to the students and connects to the problem. This provides another avenue to support the use of Mathematical Practice 3, "Construct viable arguments and critique the reasoning of others," by students critiquing an unknown group's solution. Notice that the group that determined the expression $4n - 1$ did so numerically, but in the whole-class discussion, the class is asked to make sense of this expression visually. Using the evidence she gathered in her conversation with the group, the teacher is aware that the group determined the expression from a table; however, it is important that they also be able to connect that expression back to the context of the problem. This is addressed through facilitating the whole class to critique the reasoning and justify where the expression would have come from visually. As the teacher is circulating around the groups prior to this, when expressions are determined, the students are prompted with statements like "Check to make sure you agree," which continues to foster this practice. It isn't enough for one member of the group to understand or determine an expression. There is an expectation that the members of the group support each other and work to ensure all understand the expression that was developed.

The Response

Typical areas of challenge for students related to expressions, equations, and inequalities stem from three main places: (1) modeling real-world contexts, (2) creating equivalent expressions, and (3) reasoning algebraically. To support the development of modeling real-world contexts, you should give students the opportunity to make sense of contexts and support them in developing perseverance in trying different strategies to solve problems. Students need to have the opportunity to make sense of problems first for themselves. You can accomplish this by providing them with multiple experiences with varied contexts in order to develop their ability to move between different representations, including verbal models, tables, graphs, expressions, equations, and inequalities.

In creating equivalent expressions, students sometimes struggle with using the proper order of operations. For example, consider the expression $14 - 6(3 - x)$. Students who do not have enough experiences making sense of the terms within an expression may simplify this expression as $8(3 - x)$, not understanding the proper use of the distributive property of multiplication over subtraction. They may also think that $14 - 18 - 6x$ is an equivalent expression, again having an incomplete understanding of the distributive property. This can relate back to misconceptions with order of operations with whole numbers and integers when no variables are present. Combining like terms—moving from $4t + 9t$ to $13t$ or understanding that $7p - p$ is not 7—can also be a challenge for some students. Providing students experiences with algebra tiles or balance models can help them understand the proper way to create appropriate equivalent expressions and to overcome these misconceptions. Additionally, context can be helpful. Asking students to create a context to match an expression gives a window into their thinking and provides formative assessment data to determine appropriate interventions.

Students need experiences unpacking multistep expressions in order to better understand how to create equivalent expressions. Tasks that help students make sense of the structure of expressions, terms, operations, and properties are necessary for correctly creating and identifying equivalent expressions. Linking "I have seven pencils and give one pencil to my brother; I now have six pencils" to the equation $7p - p = 6p$ will help students make sense of combining like terms. When students use sense making to link real-world contexts with symbolic representations, they are less likely to display misconceptions. Students need a progression of tasks that allow them to engage with contexts and experiences that support their development of Mathematical Practice 7, "Look for and make use of structure."

This progression of tasks begins with a shift from thinking numerically to thinking algebraically—a shift that is a critical piece of understanding in middle-grades mathematics. Students need to be able to move from specific examples involving only numbers to generalized arithmetic represented in algebraic expressions and equations. This includes building from exclusively examining tables in terms of a pattern of outputs and using recursive thinking and moving toward determining relationships between inputs and outputs explicitly. As students create tables to make sense of algebraic situations, they will often look at a pattern between the outputs to determine a recursive pattern. To generalize the arithmetic and connect to functions, however, they must see the explicit pattern related to both input and output. This can be a difficult transition for students. Context-based models, such as the bridges task (figure 3.8, page 76), help support this explicit thinking. Connecting algebraic notation and thinking to other areas including ratios and proportional relationships can be a vital intervention for students who struggle to see the connection between input and output. These students may have also had difficulty examining ratio tables and drawing conclusions based on the within relationship in the ratio.

This chapter focused on understanding and making sense of equations, expressions, and inequalities. Examining context for generalizing expressions, creating equations and inequalities, interpreting slope, and solving systems of equations lead to making sense of the mathematics in grades 6–8. The content of this chapter connects to ratios and proportions in chapter 2 and functions in chapter 4. Contexts should be carefully chosen to promote sense making of equations, expressions, and inequalities while, at the same time, addressing conceptual development of other areas of mathematics in grades 6–8, thus helping students see mathematics as a coherent, connected system of concepts.

Reflections

1. What do you feel are the key points in this chapter?

2. What challenges might you face when implementing the key ideas from this chapter? How will you overcome them?

3. What are the important features for developing an understanding of expressions, equations, and inequalities, and how will you ensure your instruction embeds the support needed for these features?

4. Select a recent lesson you have taught or observed focused on expressions, equations, or inequalities. Relate this lesson to the TQE process.

5. What changes will you make to your planning and instruction based on what you read and considered from this chapter?

CHAPTER 4

Functions

This chapter emphasizes understanding functions by unifying topics such as ratio, rate, proportionality, expressions, and equations explored in previous chapters. A fundamental understanding of function is that it is a quantitative relationship in which each input, x, results in a unique output, $f(x)$. In the middle grades, the function notation, $f(x)$, may not be required; a function can be notated using y or any other variable. For the purpose of this text and to connect to mathematics content explored in high school, function notation will be used in this chapter.

The Challenge

The initial task in this chapter (see figure 4.1) challenges you to explore your understanding of functions by asking you to create a word problem that could be modeled by the given function.

Describe a quantitative relationship that could be modeled with the function $f(x) = 2x + 20$, describe the relationship as a story, then draw a graph to represent the context you describe.

Figure 4.1: What's your story?

What story did you write? How did you determine the graph? Perhaps your graph looks something like the one in figure 4.2.

How does your graph represent the context of your story? Consider the two contexts provided in figure 4.3 (page 94). Do they match the function? How about the graph?

While both contexts support the function, neither of them is represented correctly by the graph in figure 4.2. Why? Examine each context. What is the same about them? What is different? Why is the graph not an accurate representation of either context?

The first context involves a pizza party, and the second involves a small tree. What does the input, x, represent in each scenario? In the first context, the

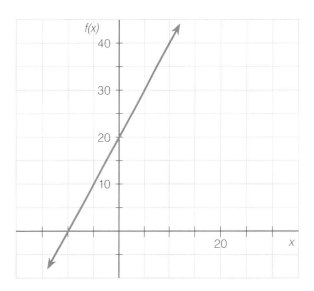

Figure 4.2: Graph for $f(x) = 2x + 20$.

input represents the number of students who read 10 books and qualified to attend the pizza party. This is a discrete variable because a fraction of a person would not make sense. Therefore, the graph in

1. You are planning a pizza party as a reward to your students for reading 10 books over the summer vacation. It will cost $20 for paper goods and another $2 for each student for the pizza. What will be the cost for the party based on the number of students who read 10 books over the summer?

2. You buy a tree that is 20 inches tall. It grows at a constant rate of 2 inches per month. How tall is the tree at any point in time after purchase?

Figure 4.3: Contexts for $f(x) = 2x + 20$.

figure 4.2 (page 93) is not appropriate for this scenario. The graph is a continuous graph and does not model the discrete context of this scenario. However, in the second context, x represents time in months, which is a continuous variable because between any two moments in time is another moment in time, and can be modeled by a continuous line.

How else is the domain, or the set of values of the inputs, restricted by the context of each scenario? The domain for each scenario is greater than or equal to zero. As stated in the previous paragraph, the first scenario is not modeled by the graph because the graph is not discrete. For both scenarios, the graphs should only represent positive values. In the second scenario, a more appropriate graph to model the situation would include a continuous line in no quadrant other than the first quadrant as illustrated in figure 4.4. Although there would also be a maximum value in the domain to indicate the tallest the tree could grow, that value would not be known until all of the data were collected.

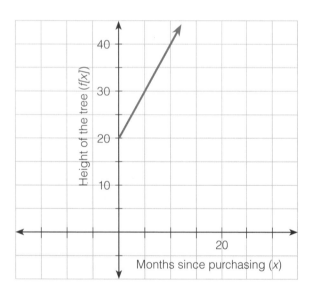

Figure 4.4: Graph for the tree-height scenario.

It is important to note that continuous graphs are often used to model discrete contexts in order to examine the relationships between the independent and dependent variables. However, as you help students make sense of functions in the middle grades, the continuous or discrete nature of the data should be made explicit when discussing graphs. Lead students to recognize when a graph does or does not accurately model the context of a problem.

With which Mathematical Practices did you engage as you investigated the task in figure 4.1 (page 93)? You most likely engaged in Mathematical Practice 4, "Model with mathematics." You did so by analyzing the function to create a real-world context and then making sure that your graph modeled both the function *and* the context. You were also likely engaged in Mathematical Practice 2, "Reason abstractly and quantitatively," as you used the function in its abstract form during graphing and then looked back to the context you created to make sure that the quantitative relationships made sense based on the scenario you provided.

The Progression

A robust understanding of functions connects the middle-grades topics of proportionality, rate of change, expressions, and equations and provides a foundation for topics learned in high school. Moreover, exploring functions affords the opportunity to link multiple representations including verbal descriptions, tables, graphs, and algebraic equations. Following is a progression for the development of understanding functions in the middle grades with links to future applications of this topic.

- Make sense of functions as rules that connect inputs and outputs.
- Use functions to model real-world situations.
- Use functions to model relationships between quantities using multiple representations.
- Define, evaluate, and compare functions.
- Represent relationships using function notation.

Although the formal teaching of functions in the middle grades does not take place until grade 8, there are many concepts explored earlier in the middle grades, including proportional relationships, expressions, and equations, that provide the foundation for making sense of functions.

Grades 6 and 7

Students in grades 6 and 7 begin to formalize their use of algebraic expressions and equations. Variables are used as a means of representing an unknown value in real-world problems that become more complex and challenging. Students expand their understanding of multiplicative reasoning by distinguishing proportional relationships from nonproportional relationships using verbal descriptions, tables, graphs, and algebraic equations. The idea of using two variables is investigated through the relationship of dependent and independent variables. Accordingly, students build on these understandings to begin their formal exploration of functions.

Grade 8

The formal teaching of functions occurs at the end of the middle grades and prepares students for continued study of functions in high school. Contexts that link the inputs of the situation to unique outputs are analyzed, thereby defining a function. These situations are explored through multiple representations, including word problems, tables of values, graphs, and equations. Analyzing different situations leads to the beginning of the development of the understanding of linear functions. Functions are represented in multiple ways, and students learn to compare functions using their understanding of multiple representations.

The Mathematics

Much of the focus on functions in the middle grades involves attention to multiple representations. Exploring multiple representations supports a deep understanding and analysis of a mathematical situation. As such, this part of the chapter will begin with the exploration of various representations used in supporting your understanding of functions, including exploring functions through different representations and linking representations together.

Exploring Functions Using a Table

When exploring a set of values in a table, you can demonstrate your reasoning about a functional relationship in many ways, including recursively or explicitly (see chapter 3). Each of these provides a different approach in understanding the mathematical relationship that you are exploring. Take a moment to make sense of the celebration task in figure 4.5 before proceeding.

Godfrey was preparing for Dutch Road Middle School's end-of-year celebration. He started the table shown to determine the cost for each student attending the celebration. How much money should he request for 75 students to attend the celebration?

Number of Students	Cost ($)
1	60
2	72
3	84
4	96
5	
6	

Figure 4.5: Celebration task.

What patterns did you notice? How did you use the patterns to help you determine the cost for any number of students who may attend? In this example, you can reason recursively by using a previous input and output to determine your subsequent input and output respectively. In fact, you may have used this reasoning to determine the cost for 5 and 6 students. As seen in figure 4.6, the cost for 3 students is $12 more than the cost for 2 students, and the cost for 4 students is $12 more than the cost for 3 students.

Using this pattern of adding $12, the cost for 5 students is the cost for 4 students plus $12, or $108. Similarly, the cost for 6 students is the cost for 5 students plus $12, or $120. This way of reasoning shows that the constant difference between consecutive terms is $12. How could you use this reasoning to determine the cost for 75 students? Although any number of students attending the party can be found, this way of reasoning presents an inefficient strategy because you would need to derive every previous output in the function table prior to determining the cost for 75 students.

Number of Students	Cost ($)
1	60
2	72
3	84
4	96
5	
6	
. . .	
75	

+1 between 1 and 2, +1 between 2 and 3, +1 between 3 and 4; +12 between 60 and 72, +12 between 72 and 84, +12 between 84 and 96.

Figure 4.6: Recursive thinking in a function table.

How could this table be used in a more efficient way? This question connects to the conversation from chapter 3 about explicit thinking. A more efficient way to reason with the table and determine the cost for 75 students is to come to a generalization for any number of students who will attend the party. To do so, you must determine an explicit expression that relates any input value of students to determine its unique output, or cost. You can use your recursive thinking to expand your initial thinking about rate of change and determine an explicit equation. For instance, as the number of students increases by 1, the cost increases by $12. This indicates that the rate of change of the function, or slope of the graphed line of the function, is $12 per student. How do you get a generalized function from this table? The rate of change is $12 per student, but the function is not $f(x) = 12x$. What is the generalized function? You can examine the table output in order to determine that the cost, $f(x)$, for any number of students, x, is $f(x) = 12x + 48$. Take a moment to look back at the task in figure 4.5 and determine how this function can be generated from the table. Consider how you can help students think about the cost of no students attending the celebration and how that discussion will set the stage for thinking about the graph and the y-intercept. Notice that while the 48 is also a multiple of 12, it does not have a direct impact in determining the rate of change. Think about how this choice of the value of the y-intercept can help uncover possible misconceptions of students.

Exploring Functions Using a Graph

Another representation that allows you to explore functions is a graph. Consider figure 4.7. How does the graph help you see the relationship in ways that other representations—including a verbal description, table, or equation—do not?

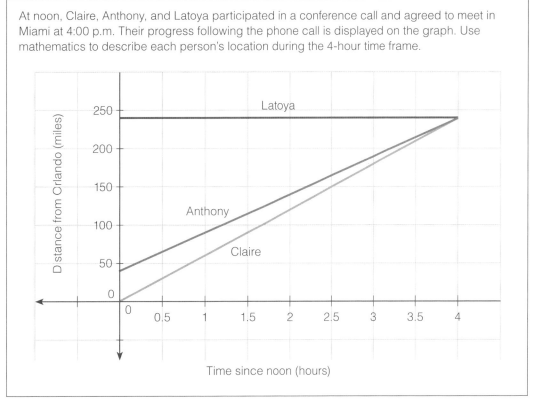

At noon, Claire, Anthony, and Latoya participated in a conference call and agreed to meet in Miami at 4:00 p.m. Their progress following the phone call is displayed on the graph. Use mathematics to describe each person's location during the 4-hour time frame.

Figure 4.7: Meeting in Miami.

What observations about the graph did you make? How can you use mathematics to describe what is happening for each person? Which measure in the relationship is the independent variable, and which is the dependent variable? Time is not dependent on anything, so the time in hours is the independent variable and is represented on the x-axis. The number of miles from Orlando, or distance, is dependent on time and is the dependent variable. It is represented on the y-axis. The values for the number of hours driven and distance can only be positive, so the graph only uses the first quadrant, where the values of all variables are positive.

When looking at the graphs of the three functions, you see that each function is represented as a straight line. This means that they each can be represented by a linear equation. You also should notice that each line has a different slope. This observation is key in comparing the quantitative relationships being graphed. What does it mean that Latoya's graph is a horizontal line? Latoya's distance traveled does not change during the four hours, meaning that the line representing her location is a constant linear function with a slope of 0. In this case, $L(t) = 240$. What does this mean in the context of the problem? The horizontal line indicates that Latoya is not traveling; her distance from Orlando is not changing. It is likely that she was in Miami when the call ended.

Where does the line representing Claire's trip begin? How steep is it? Her trip begins at 0 miles, so she traveled the entire 240 miles over the 4 hours. This indicates her speed, or slope, was 60 miles per hour (see chapter 3 for a discussion of slope). Since Claire's trip started at distance zero and she maintained a constant rate of speed, her relationship is directly proportional and is represented by the equation $C(t) = 60t$.

What about Anthony? What do you notice about Anthony's graph? How is it different from Latoya's graph? How is it different from Claire's graph? The y-intercept for Anthony's graph occurs at 40 miles. This can be considered Anthony's head start compared to Claire. As you continue to examine Anthony's graph, you can see that he traveled 200 miles in 4 hours, so he traveled at a constant speed of 50 miles per hour, which is his slope. The linear function representing Anthony's trip, then, would be $A(t) = 50t + 40$.

In the end, you should realize that all three individuals were in the same place exactly four hours after the call ended. What are some other questions you may consider related to these graphs? Who traveled the longest distance? According to the graph, Claire traveled the longest distance during the 4 hours after the phone call. What does it mean that Anthony's graph is less steep than Claire's graph? This would mean that Anthony traveled more slowly than Claire. Encouraging students to pose and answer these types of questions from graphs and other representations is useful in helping them use graphs as sense-making tools. Students will learn how various representations may lead them to consider multiple aspects of a situation and the benefits of using and connecting different representations to create and answer different questions.

Linking Representations

One way to link the various representations of a function is by beginning with an algebraic equation and making sense of the functional relationship (see figure 4.8). For many teachers, this was the way functions were initially explored. That is, you may have been introduced to functions without context. Functions should be connected to context early in instruction to keep the focus on sense making. It is also important to create context for a function represented symbolically to make sense of its meaning. Complete the task in figure 4.8 before proceeding.

Create a word problem to represent $f(x) = 15 - 3x$. Make a table and a graph to represent your context.

Figure 4.8: Connecting representations.

Why is it important to know different representations? What information does one representation provide more clearly than another? Making tables helps highlight specific values in the quantitative relationship, while graphs focus on a visual representation of the change in the values. The context influences the values that make sense with the given function versus those that do not. Was the context you created continuous or discrete? Did your context correspond with the values you used in your table and those you graphed? Perhaps you used $x = -1$ in your table. Is it a value that makes sense with the context you chose?

Determining contexts where values exist in quadrants other than quadrant I is challenging. If your original context did not correspond to the graph existing in quadrants other than quadrant I, try to come up with a different context that would include values in another quadrant before proceeding. One is provided in figure 4.9.

At 5:00 p.m., the temperature outside is 15 degrees Fahrenheit. The temperature drops at a constant rate of 3 degrees per hour. What is the temperature at any time after 5:00 p.m.?

Figure 4.9: Context to move beyond quadrant I.

Was your context similar to the one provided in figure 4.9? What would the graph look like for the context provided here? See figure 4.10.

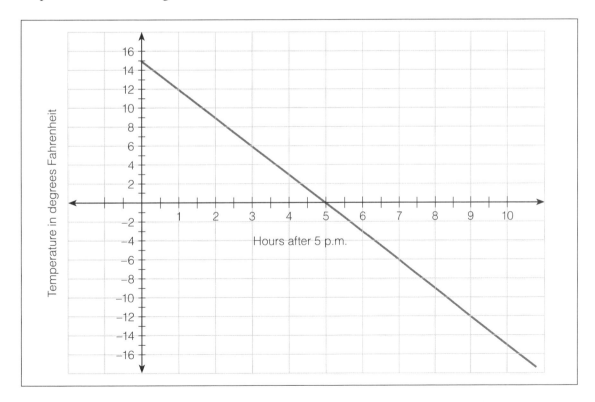

Figure 4.10: Graph of temperature context.

What values would make sense for this context? In this case, it makes sense for the temperature to be negative, thus including quadrant IV in the graph. Students need to be challenged to think about contexts that are supported by graphs in quadrants beyond quadrant I. This flexible thinking reinforces their understanding of quantitative relationships and functions.

The Classroom

Now that you have explored your own thinking about functions, you will explore what this could look like in the classroom. The following videos provide some important insight into student thinking about functional relationships. In the first video, students make sense of multiple representations of functions. In this video, they explore tables, graphs, and equations. You are encouraged to watch the video in its entirety before proceeding.

www.solution-tree.com/Connecting_Representations
_of_Functions

Now that you have had the opportunity to watch students actively engaged in making sense of these representations, what are your thoughts? Perhaps you noticed that the teacher rarely *gives* answers but rather elicits them from students. The teacher asks specific questions to gauge student thinking. He is more concerned with how students are thinking about the representations and how they are linking them together than whether they achieve a particular result.

As the teacher spends time with various groups, what did you notice? What are the students doing? Perhaps you noticed the types of questions the teacher asks each group. He begins by asking the first group what they are doing. This group is struggling with matching the graphs; he supports their thinking and their group collaboration through questioning. Asking the other group members to provide suggestions for making sense of the graphs and asking students to re-voice group members' contributions are helpful strategies that provide data to the teacher and support the group collaboration.

What did you notice about the strategies used by the students? Are there common strategies? What different strategies are present? Often, it is easier to provide students with one strategy and ask them to apply that strategy. For example, in this case, the teacher could have said, "Start with the equation, plug in points to fill in the table, and plot them on the graph." This would take less time; however, it would remove the role of the students to actively think about the problem. Instead, by giving the task to sort the different representations, students develop multiple strategies to determine how the tables, graphs, and equations are connected. This provides a richer foundation and a deeper understanding of functional relationships and representations. Some students begin with the table and test the points in the equations. Others begin with the graph and see if the points in the table are represented on the graph. Still others begin with the equation and make sense of the table and graph based on each equation. These multiple ways of thinking are as important as the ways that the table, graph, and equation represent different facets of the same functional relationship.

In this video, the students engage in Mathematical Practice 1, "Make sense of problems and persevere in solving them." As students attempt to make sense of one or more representations, they need perseverance to complete the task. The teacher's questions to students as they work in their small groups help guide the students to make sense of the problem.

In the next video, you will explore high school students interpreting a graph that involves a race between father and son. We encourage you to watch the video clip in its entirety before proceeding.

www.solution-tree.com/Interpreting_Graphs_to
_Create_Context

Now that you have had the opportunity to watch these students engaged in making sense of a graph, what are your thoughts? What insights did you gain regarding student thinking? How do students use their prior knowledge of functions to make sense of this problem?

The focus of instruction on functions can be limited to generating graphs from tables and equations. It is important for students to interpret graphs accurately and create contexts that match graphs. As students interpret the graph in this lesson, misconceptions arise. One misconception involves how students interpret the distance-time graph as a representation of the situation. Some students interpret the positive slope between distance and time to mean that the *speed* is increasing. Because the line on the graph is getting higher, the person must be running faster.

How does the teacher identify this misconception? What does she do the first time it is discovered? Initially, when asking a group to tell her what they are doing, one of the students says that the father and son meet at four seconds. Then the student determines that the son starts to go faster and the father slows down. In another group, discussion revolves around the same misconception. One student says the father and son are accelerating, and another student disagrees, stating that the lines are straight, so their pace is constant. This same student, however, then goes on to say that after four seconds, the son starts to run faster.

What in the graph leads to these statements? At the start of the race, the graph of the father's line is "above" the son's line. At four seconds, the lines representing the father and son intersect. At that point in time, the son passes the father, so his line is above the father's line. This leads to misinterpreting the graph as the son is now running faster since his graph is above the father's graph. The teacher is aware of this misconception and uses a formative assessment process to see whether it is present in the student's thinking. Since it appears in multiple groups, she facilitates a whole-class discussion to address this misconception. Through eliciting student responses in the whole-class discussion, the teacher is able to support students in making sense of what is actually happening in the graph. As the graph goes "higher," it means they have run farther, not faster. The students identify that the pace each was running was constant, and their speed didn't change even after the intersection point. This is important for students to understand. It would have been easy for the teacher to tell them this directly; however, by asking carefully crafted questions, students are able to make sense of it for themselves, and they are much less likely to make that error again. In this way, a common error is used as a springboard for learning.

The teacher is fostering Mathematical Practice 2, "Reason abstractly and quantitatively," and Mathematical Practice 4, "Model with mathematics." By receiving a task that is graphical in nature, students have to contextualize the problem by interpreting what is occurring at various points in the race. Students examine the graph to make sense of the context and then return to the graph to verify that their context is accurate. They also connect the graphical representation to a real-world scenario.

TQE Process

At this point, it may be helpful to watch the second video (page 101) again and pay close attention to the tasks, questioning, and opportunities to collect evidence of student learning. The TQE process can help you frame your observations. Teachers who have a deep understanding of the mathematics they teach:

- Select appropriate *tasks* to support identified learning goals
- Facilitate productive *questioning* during instruction to engage students in Mathematical Practices
- Collect and use student *evidence* in the formative assessment process during instruction

The *task* chosen for this lesson involves distance-time graphs and connecting graphs to real-world situations. The teacher is aware that misconceptions exist when interpreting distance-time graphs, and the task and planned questions are designed to identify these misconceptions. In particular, she is aware that many students interpret distance-time graphs as depicting the event as speed-time or location-time instead of distance-time graphs. In other words, as the graph goes "up," this means the person is running faster or is running uphill. This misconception was apparent in the classroom discussion, and the task provided an avenue for the teacher to address this misconception in a way that was meaningful to the students.

Perhaps you noticed the types of *questions* the teacher asks the small groups as she circulates among them. How do her questions support student thinking and facilitate small-group and individual learning? She does not give answers early on, nor does she provide strategies. She instead asks questions that require the *students* to explain their thinking. The focus is on the students and how they are making sense of the problem. Asking questions like "What are you doing?" provides a way for the teacher to learn about student reasoning and facilitate the thinking of the students without taking the focus off of the students. When students ask questions or respond to the teacher's questions, she replies by asking additional questions such as "Where are they when the race starts?" or "Does the father's pace change?" The impetus for these questions remains on facilitating student thinking. The teacher asks additional questions to engage all members of the group in productive discussion, and these questions support the interactions of the group even after she moves to another group. Asking questions like "What does he mean?" provides ways for students to interpret and respond to each other's thinking. In one case, a student mentions that the son is accelerating faster than the father. The teacher asks the group what that means, which prompts another student to say, "That's what I wanted to know!" This provides an avenue for the students to engage in Mathematical Practice 3, "Construct viable arguments and critique the reasoning of others," by making sense of each other's thinking and productively discussing why ideas are correct or incorrect. The teacher's response of "Then you have a question for your group" also serves to promote productive talk from student to student.

The students provide *evidence* of their level of understanding—and their misconceptions—as they engage in the task. Again, through thoughtful planning and questioning of students and eliciting their thinking, the teacher identifies several misconceptions related to the graph. These include misinterpreting the points on the graph and misinterpreting the slope as acceleration instead of speed. By asking pointed questions, the teacher is able to gather formative assessment data that then drive the whole-class discussion. As the teacher brings the students back together for a discussion regarding this problem, she is able to use the data she collected in small groups to guide the direction of the lesson. She knows that some students misinterpreted what was occurring at the start of the race, so she is mindful to ask about it during the whole-class discussion. Instead of providing a judgment of correctness, she prompts the students to justify their answers using the graph. She knows the interpretation of distance as speed is a misconception, so she makes sure to ask the whole class about the speed at various points in time on the graph, particularly after the intersection point. She is careful to elicit the misconception and to provide questions and discussion that help students determine what is mathematically correct.

The Response

Despite the opportunity to link representations, many middle-grades students struggle with the fact that a function can be represented in multiple ways and that each representation provides a perspective that is helpful in understanding the mathematical relationship. Instead, they often explore the concept procedurally, considering the word problem and representing the situation in different ways, beginning with an equation, then substituting values into the equation to build a table, followed by graphing the values from the table as coordinate pairs. Regrettably, this leads students to think a function is always best represented by an equation, whereas the other representations are simply byproducts or are ignored completely. This conclusion also occurs when instruction parallels this order of exploration. It is efficient to give students procedures to follow; these procedures often begin with the equation and then move to other representations. Following procedures without meaning does not support students to make sense of functions and the value of multiple representations. Instead, selecting meaningful tasks that provide avenues for making sense of each representation and how representations connect together becomes critically important. It is also important for students to reason independently with each type of representation and make sense of why different representations are meaningful in different contexts. If students are struggling to make sense of graphical representations, for example, providing tasks that ask students to reason only with the graph can provide insight into their thinking and potential misconceptions. Some students will need to revisit how graphs are created and what they represent in context while others need to revisit how tables and graphs are connected. This revisiting can connect to ratio tables and generalizing expressions and equations as discussed in chapters 2 and 3.

Students in grade 8 must be challenged to explore functions thoroughly by making connections among verbal, tabular, graphic, and algebraic representations. Doing so will help solidify their understanding. However, attention also needs to be given to support students to develop an accurate definition of functions. Students need to make sense of and apply the idea that functions map every input to exactly one output. This is an area where students often struggle. For example, when looking at a graph of a function, students often incorrectly conclude that linear equations that result in a horizontal line on the coordinate grid are not functions. This misconception often surfaces when students examine graphs like the one representing Latoya's trip in figure 4.7 (page 97). It is important to provide examples of constant functions during instruction so students learn that functions can have the same output for every input value. If explored in context, students can be pressed into expressing what is happening; in this case, they would determine that Latoya is not traveling during the four hours, so each input has only one output—that of 240 miles. As a result, by having their misconceptions challenged, the students can expand their understanding of a function not solely as a one-to-one relationship but one that can also include a many-to-one relationship. Further exploration of functions occurs in *Making Sense of Mathematics for Teaching High School* (Nolan et al., 2016).

Students will benefit from opportunities to view mathematics as something to explore. As such, it is helpful to leverage students' understanding of topics like ratio, rate, proportionality, expressions, and equations studied earlier in the middle grades as a means to explore functions. Doing so will help students build a deep understanding between the four representations of functions as illustrated throughout the chapter and understand the connectedness and coherence of mathematics.

Reflections

1. What do you feel are the key points in this chapter?

2. What challenges might you face when implementing the key ideas from this chapter? How will you overcome them?

3. What are the important features for developing an understanding of functions, and how will you ensure your instruction embeds the support needed for these features?

4. Select a recent lesson you have taught or observed focused on functions. Relate this lesson to the TQE process.

5. What changes will you make to your planning and instruction based on what you read and considered from this chapter?

CHAPTER 5

Measurement and Geometry

In this chapter we unpack big ideas in measurement and geometry in order to make sense of concepts as well as formulas for area, surface area, and volume of various simple and complex shapes. Teaching geometric measurement with depth involves making sense of why these formulas work, connecting them to algebraic reasoning within the coordinate plane, and applying geometric measurement to real-world scenarios. Geometry concepts also include examining angles, transformations, congruency and similarity, and the Pythagorean theorem. As learning progresses through grades 6–8, the contexts and applications of measurement and geometry become more complex.

The Challenge

Take a few minutes to make sense of a formula for the area of a trapezoid (see figure 5.1). Pay particular attention to how you develop your formula.

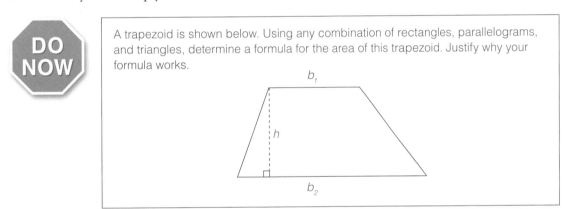

Figure 5.1: Area of a trapezoid task.

How could you determine a formula for the area of the trapezoid in figure 5.1? How did decomposing the shape help you determine a formula? You may have started by dividing the trapezoid into a rectangle and two triangles as shown in figure 5.2.

How might figure 5.2 help you determine a formula for the area of the original trapezoid? How can you determine the area of each part? This decomposition may leave you feeling like you don't have enough information to determine the area formula. The information is there; the challenge is to make sense of how to find the area of the triangles.

The formula for the area of a rectangle is base times height, so in this case, $A_{rect} = b_1 h$. Why do you use b_1 for the base of

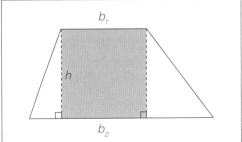

Figure 5.2: Trapezoid divided into a rectangle and two triangles.

the rectangle? Since b_2 is the longer base (and includes the bases of the triangles), you should use b_1—the shorter side—to determine the area of the rectangle.

How can you find the area of the triangles? You may be tempted to take the difference between b_2 and b_1 and divide it in half to find the base of each triangle. Do you know whether the difference in the bases of the trapezoid is divided evenly between the two triangles? This is only the case with isosceles trapezoids. You are not given information to indicate this trapezoid is isosceles, so you cannot assume that the base of each triangle is half the difference of the bases of the trapezoid. How can you find the area of the triangles? Consider the decomposed trapezoid in figure 5.3. Copy the trapezoid onto a separate piece of paper and cut it apart. If you cut the rectangle out of the middle of the trapezoid, what can you do with the two triangles to make sense of finding the area?

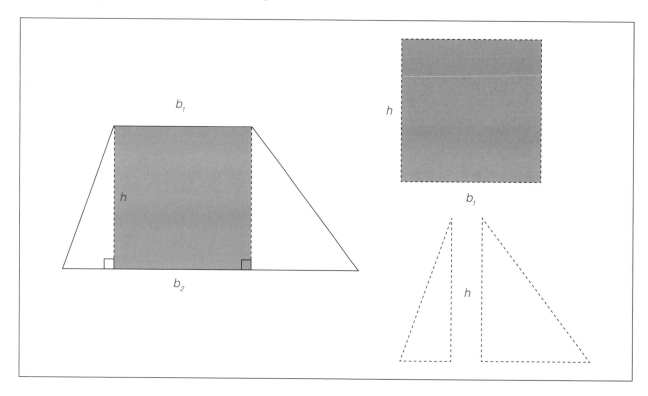

Figure 5.3: Decomposing the trapezoid into a rectangle and triangles.

The two triangles have the same height. How might composing the two triangles together into a larger triangle help you determine the area of the triangles? What would be the base of this newly composed triangle? Figure 5.4 provides a visual of the original and newly composed shapes.

The base of the newly created triangle is the difference in the bases of the trapezoid. The area of the triangle in this case is $A_{tri} = \frac{1}{2}(b_2 - b_1)h$. You now have all of the components necessary to determine the area of the entire trapezoid. Since you decomposed the trapezoid into a rectangle and a newly composed triangle, you can add those two expressions together to determine the area of the trapezoid so that $A_{trap} = A_{rect} + A_{tri} = b_1 h + \frac{1}{2}(b_2 - b_1)h$. It is likely that this formula is different from the formula for the area of a trapezoid with which you are most accustomed. Is there a way to link that formula with the formula

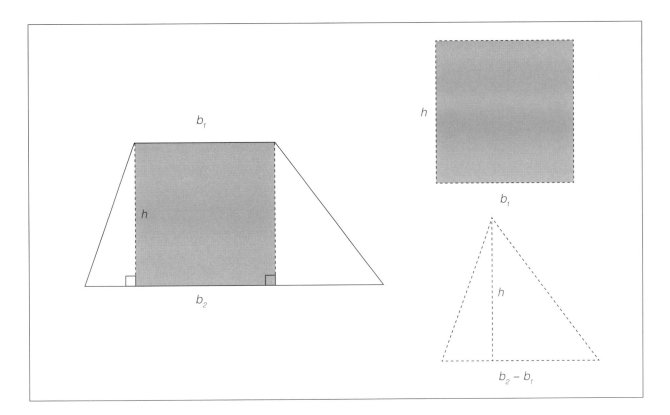

Figure 5.4: Combining the two triangles together into one triangle.

you have just created? A common formula for the area of a trapezoid is $A_{trap} = \frac{1}{2}(b_1 + b_2)h$. How can you justify that your formula is equivalent to this formula? Think back to chapter 3 and how you determined equivalent expressions and equations (see figure 5.5).

Figure 5.5 shows that the two formulas are, in fact, equivalent. What other ways might you determine the area of a trapezoid? Perhaps you are thinking about decomposing the trapezoid in alternative ways or adding different shapes to the trapezoid to make sense of

$A_{trap} = b_1 h + \frac{1}{2}(b_2 - b_1)h$	Derived Formula
$= b_1 h + \frac{1}{2}b_2 h - \frac{1}{2}b_1 h$	Distribute $\frac{1}{2}$ and h
$= [b_1 + \frac{1}{2}b_2 - \frac{1}{2}b_1]h$	Factor out h
$= [\frac{1}{2}b_1 + \frac{1}{2}b_2]h$	Combine b_1 terms
$= \frac{1}{2}(b_1 + b_2)h$	Factor out $\frac{1}{2}$

Figure 5.5: Showing two formulas for the area of a trapezoid are equivalent.

the formula. Is one method more efficient than another? Consider three additional methods to make sense of the area formula for a trapezoid shown in figure 5.6 (page 108). Before reading on, connect each method to a formula.

Method One

In this case, a line segment is drawn from point C parallel to $\overline{AB}$. This creates parallelogram $ABCF$ and $\triangle CDF$. Segment $\overline{AD}$ can be decomposed into $\overline{AF}$ and $\overline{FD}$. Since the opposite sides of a parallelogram are congruent, the length of b_2 is separated into b_1 and $(b_2 - b_1)$, so $AF = b_1$ and $FD = (b_2 - b_1)$. Algebraically,

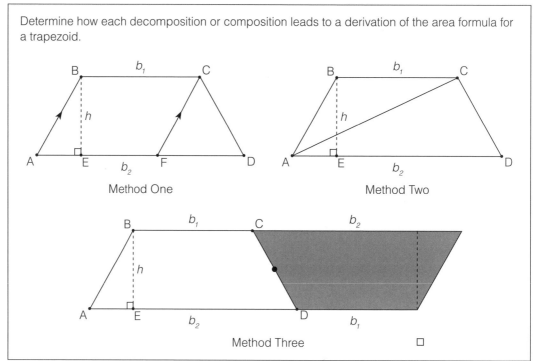

Determine how each decomposition or composition leads to a derivation of the area formula for a trapezoid.

Figure 5.6: Three methods for finding the formula for the area of a trapezoid.

the resulting formula is equivalent to the first situation of decomposing the trapezoid into a rectangle and two triangles. This is because the area of a rectangle and the area of a parallelogram are both base times height, and so, $A_{trap} = A_{par} + A_{tri} = b_1 h + \frac{1}{2}(b_2 - b_1)h$. How does this method compare to the method you chose to use? You may notice that it is somewhat easier to see the base of the triangle when the trapezoid is decomposed into a parallelogram and a triangle rather than into a rectangle and two triangles.

Method Two

What is the difference between method two and method one? In method one, the trapezoid is decomposed into a parallelogram and a triangle. In method two, the trapezoid is decomposed into two triangles by drawing $\overline{AC}$. How might the triangles be described? Both of these triangles, $\triangle ABC$ and $\triangle ACD$, are obtuse triangles. Using descriptive labels provides a useful review of shape names and categories in the context of making sense of the problem. What are the base and height of each of these triangles? It is sometimes difficult to see the height of an obtuse triangle; however, the height of the trapezoid is the same as the height of each of the triangles (see figure 5.7).

The height is always drawn perpendicular to the base. In cases of obtuse triangles, like $\triangle ABC$ (or triangle 1), the height drawn from point A intersects the line containing $\overline{BC}$. The height of $\triangle ACD$ (or triangle 2) is drawn from C perpendicular to $\overline{AD}$. These heights, however, are equal and are the same as the height of the trapezoid. The area of each triangle can be found and then added together to find the area of the trapezoid. This can be represented as $A_{trap} = A_{tri1} + A_{tri2} = \frac{1}{2}b_1 h + \frac{1}{2}b_2 h$. This formula for the area of the trapezoid can be transformed into the equivalent formula with which you may be most familiar through the use of the distributive property of multiplication over addition. Both terms have a factor of ½ and a factor of h. Factoring these out gives $A_{trap} = \frac{1}{2}(b_1 + b_2)h$.

Method Three

What is different about method three? In the first two methods, the area of the trapezoid was determined by decomposing the trapezoid into other shapes such as parallelograms and triangles. In method three, composition, or putting shapes together, is used. The trapezoid is rotated 180° about a center of rotation that is the midpoint of a side that is not one of the bases (in this case, $\overline{CD}$). The resulting pre-image (the original trapezoid) and image (the figure that is the result of the transformation) create the shape represented in method three of figure 5.6. Since the pre-image is rotated 180°, b_1 is now on the bottom of the image and b_2 is now on the top. The newly composed shape is a parallelogram. What are the dimensions of this new parallelogram? The base of the parallelogram is the sum

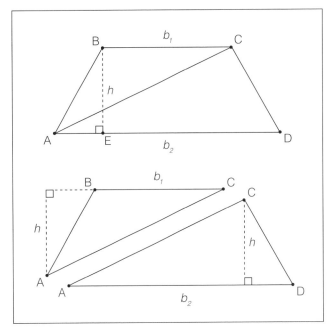

Figure 5.7: Trapezoid decomposed into two triangles.

of the bases of the trapezoid, or $b_1 + b_2$. The height of the parallelogram is the same as the height of the trapezoid. What is the area of the parallelogram? The area of a parallelogram is the product of its base and associated height, so the area of the parallelogram is $A_{par} = (b_1 + b_2)h$. How does the area of the parallelogram relate to the area of the trapezoid? The parallelogram is made up of two congruent trapezoids, so the area of one of the trapezoids is equal to one-half the area of the parallelogram. Therefore, $A_{trap} = \frac{1}{2}(b_1 + b_2)h$. This last method is quite efficient in reaching a simplified expression; however, any of these techniques will determine the area formula of a trapezoid.

As you considered this task, with which Mathematical Practices were you engaged? One was Mathematical Practice 3, "Construct viable arguments and critique the reasoning of others." Through the process of examining the area of a trapezoid, various methods resulted in different strategies of how to determine the formula. As you examined your own method and compared it to other methods, you were constructing arguments as to why your method was appropriate. At the same time, you were critiquing the reasoning of others by making sense of the alternate methods and how they might be similar to or different from your method.

You also engaged in Mathematical Practice 7, "Look for and make use of structure," in that you used the structure and properties of shapes to make sense of finding the area of an unknown shape, in this case, a trapezoid. By exploring the geometric structure of the trapezoid, the areas of rectangles, triangles, and parallelograms were used to make sense of the area of a trapezoid. The structure of equations and expressions also supported your viable arguments when you found equivalent expressions. This use of other topics in mathematics helps reinforce the connections between ideas in mathematics and the progression of those ideas throughout the grades.

An Alternate Method

Consider one more method for determining the area of this trapezoid (see figure 5.8). In this case, the trapezoid is transformed into a rectangle. How is this rectangle created? How can you determine the base and height of this rectangle?

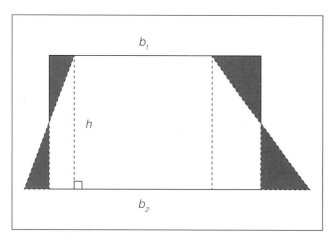

Figure 5.8: Transforming a trapezoid into a rectangle.

The rectangle is created by first decomposing the trapezoid into a rectangle and two triangles similar to the decomposition in figure 5.3 (page 106). Next, the base of each decomposed triangle is bisected and two new smaller triangles are formed. These triangles are rotated 180° about the midpoint of the hypotenuse for each original triangle. The rotated smaller triangles form rectangles with the part of the triangles that were not rotated. These rectangles are composed with the rectangle from the trapezoid to make a larger rectangle. How, then, is the length of the newly formed base of the rectangle determined? Since you have rotated part of the base of each triangle to the opposite base of the trapezoid, the length of the opposite sides of the newly formed rectangle is the mean of the two bases of the original trapezoid, or $\frac{1}{2}(b_1 + b_2)$. Using the formula for the area of a rectangle leads to the formula $A_{trap} = \frac{1}{2}(b_1 + b_2)h$. This strategy provides another way that you can make sense of the formula for the area of a trapezoid.

The Progression

The formal development of understanding of measurement and geometry begins in kindergarten with students making sense of shapes and spatial relationships. As students progress throughout the elementary grades, the complexity and type of shapes change. In the middle grades, students apply the properties learned in the elementary grades to a variety of more complex shapes and in new ways. Following is a progression within measurement and geometry in grades 6–8.

- Compose and decompose two-dimensional shapes to find area.

- Apply area understanding to find surface area of three-dimensional shapes.

- Determine formulas and use them to find volume of three-dimensional shapes.

- Connect the concepts of perimeter, area, surface area, and volume.

- Use and apply properties of angles and parallel lines.

- Determine congruency and apply ratio and proportional relationships to scale drawings and similarity.

- Transform two-dimensional shapes by translating, reflecting, rotating, and dilating.

- Make sense of the distance formula and the Pythagorean theorem.

As students progress through elementary-grades and middle-grades mathematics, composing and decomposing shapes deepens their understanding of area and leads to the development of understanding surface area and volume. Parallel to the development of understanding geometric measurement is the development of underlying geometry concepts, which continually connects to other areas of mathematics, such as fractions, ratios, and proportions. Students begin to use the coordinate plane for representing algebraic models and connect to similar triangles, scale factor, and slope. Properties and classifications of shapes are expanded to include properties of parallel lines, congruent and similar shapes, and the Pythagorean theorem.

Grade 6

As students transition to the middle grades, they bring the conceptual development of the meaning of area as the number of square units used to cover a shape completely with no gaps or overlaps, particularly applied to rectangles and connected to multiplication and rectangular arrays. In grade 6, students build on their understandings from the elementary grades to determine the areas of different shapes, including triangles (right and otherwise), additional special quadrilaterals (kite, parallelogram, rhombus, and trapezoid), and other polygons. Students apply their understandings of area to solve real-world problems. Shapes are also drawn on the coordinate plane, and this structure is used to determine dimensions in order to solve problems.

Similarly, student understanding of volume from the elementary grades is primarily related to the number of cubic units that fill a prism. This understanding is expanded in the middle grades to right rectangular prisms with fractional dimensions (students determine area of rectangles involving fractional dimensions in grade 5). Students examine nets of three-dimensional solids, including prisms and pyramids, and develop an understanding of surface area.

Grade 7

Geometric understandings in grade 7 connect to prior knowledge of shapes and proportional reasoning to create scale drawings and to determine dimensions from scale drawings. Students use their understanding of shapes to consider which shapes can be formed based on given information, including determining when the given information allows for only one possible shape and when multiple shapes can be created from that information. For example, what shapes can be drawn that have two sets of parallel sides? What if the shapes are limited to quadrilaterals? How does that change what shapes can be included? Students' spatial visualization is further developed as they find two-dimensional cross sections of three-dimensional objects.

Geometric measurement is enhanced in grade 7 by applying understandings of area and circumference of circles and area of shapes composed of triangles, quadrilaterals, and other polygons to real-world problems. Volume and surface area of prisms are also determined. Understanding angles and their properties expands from earlier exposure in the elementary grades and is applied to types of angles including supplementary, complementary, vertical, and adjacent angles. Also, algebraic expressions and equations are applied to solving problems generated by geometric properties, such as creating an equation from two angles that are supplementary and are given as algebraic expressions rather than numerical values.

Grade 8

Geometry in grade 8 transitions to understanding congruency and similarity by applying and making sense of transformational geometry, including translations, reflections, rotations, and dilations. The angles of a triangle are examined, and the angles formed by parallel lines and transversals are investigated to make sense of other geometric properties and to solve problems. The Pythagorean theorem is introduced and examined as it applies to right triangles. Students in grade 8 prove the Pythagorean theorem and its converse and use them to solve problems. Geometric measurement is expanded in grade 8 to include the volume of cones, cylinders, and spheres.

The Mathematics

In grades 6–8, the big ideas of measurement include area, surface area, and volume. In addition, you will explore transformational geometry, angles and parallel lines, and the Pythagorean theorem through the tasks in this chapter. While there are additional aspects of measurement studied in the middle grades, including linear measurement and distance, we do not address them in depth in this book.

Investigating Area

The focus on area begins in the elementary grades and transitions into grades 6–8 by applying understanding of area to new shapes. Students investigate covering two-dimensional shapes in order to define area as the number of square units that the shape covers. In the elementary grades, students apply understandings of multiplication to make sense of area of rectangles as an application of rectangular arrays. They apply Mathematical Practice 7, "Look for and make use of structure," to the rectangular array to make sense of the area of a rectangle with the same dimensions. For example, a rectangular array for $2 \cdot 4$ is two rows with four in each row, or two groups of four, as shown in figure 5.9 using squares.

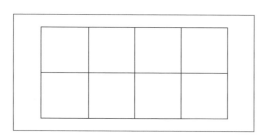

Figure 5.9: Rectangular array for 2 × 4.

Students in the elementary grades use rectangular arrays as a model for multiplication, so the extension to area is natural. Since an array for two rows of four squares is eight squares, the area of a region that is two units by four units is eight square units. This can be found by counting the number of square units in the array; however, as the dimensions of a rectangle get larger or when the dimensions include fractions of units, counting the number of squares becomes cumbersome. For this reason, a generalized formula for the area of a rectangle is needed. The creation of a generalized formula is similar to the creation of algebraic expressions and equations to represent sequences in chapter 3. In this case, the algebraic equation is a formula for the area of a rectangle. Since the angles in a rectangle are right angles, the dimensions of a rectangle are also the base (b) and the height (h). You can then generalize the area of a rectangle to be $A_{rect} = bh$.

This understanding of the area of a rectangle can then be used to make sense of the formulas for the area of parallelograms and triangles. Take a moment to consider the task in figure 5.10, and determine how you might find a formula for the area of a parallelogram.

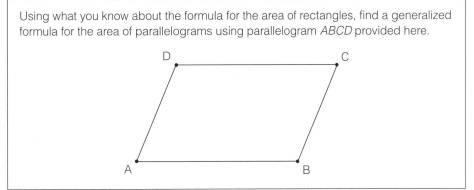

Using what you know about the formula for the area of rectangles, find a generalized formula for the area of parallelograms using parallelogram *ABCD* provided here.

Figure 5.10: Area of parallelogram task.

A parallelogram is defined as a four-sided shape, or quadrilateral, with two sets of parallel sides, in this case, $\overline{AD} \parallel \overline{BC}$ and $\overline{AB} \parallel \overline{DC}$. How could decomposing the parallelogram help you derive the formula for the area of a parallelogram? What shape would you want to create from the parallelogram? You might decompose the parallelogram as shown in figure 5.11. How could you compose the two pieces to create a rectangle?

If you were to copy this figure, cut it along $\overline{FG}$ and translate polygon *AGFD* horizontally to the right, you could rename the translated points *J* and *H*. You will compose the rectangle *GJHF* (see figure 5.12).

How do you know this is a rectangle? One property of a parallelogram is that opposite sides are parallel. Also, a rectangle can be described as a parallelogram with right angles at each vertex. Since the line was drawn at a right angle to the base of the parallelogram, the new shape, *GJHF* must be a rectangle. You know how to find the area of a rectangle, so how does this relate to finding the area of the original parallelogram? The area of the rectangle and the area of the parallelogram are equivalent, so $A_{par} = bh$.

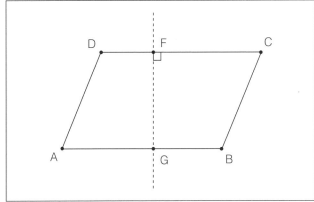

Figure 5.11: Decomposing a parallelogram.

How would you determine the base and height of the parallelogram? Is the height of the parallelogram the same as the length of the side of the parallelogram? Examine figure 5.12 again. The height of the rectangle is the length of $\overline{GF}$. Note that this is not the same as the length of $\overline{AD}$. How does the base of the parallelogram compare to the base of the rectangle? They actually are the

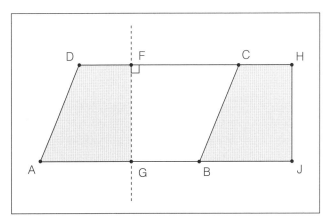

Figure 5.12: Composing a rectangle.

same length. Why? When the parallelogram was cut and the rectangle was composed, the portion of $\overline{AB}$ cut off ($\overline{AG}$) was then added back to the right of $\overline{GB}$ ($\overline{BJ}$), creating $\overline{GJ}$. In addition, either side of the parallelogram can be chosen as the base; the height is perpendicular to that chosen base, and the height of the parallelogram is the length of that perpendicular segment from the base to its parallel side (see figure 5.13).

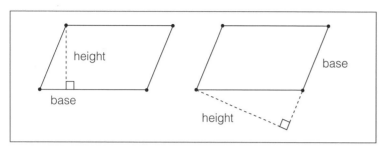

Figure 5.13: Base and associated height options for a parallelogram.

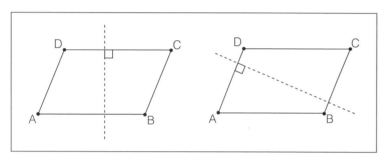

Figure 5.14: Cutting a parallelogram in different ways.

Consider the line where the original parallelogram was cut (see figure 5.11, page 113). Does it matter how this line is drawn in relation to the side of the parallelogram? In order to use the properties of rectangles, you must create a right angle; therefore, this line must be drawn perpendicular to the base of the parallelogram. It also must intersect both the parallel sides—in this case, $\overline{AB}$ and $\overline{DC}$. What if this line had been drawn perpendicular to $\overline{AD}$ and $\overline{BC}$ instead? While a line for this purpose could be drawn to either side of the parallelogram (see figure 5.14), it must be perpendicular in order to use the properties of a rectangle to create a formula for the area of a parallelogram.

Once the area of a parallelogram is determined, areas of other shapes can be examined. The formulas for the areas of triangles, trapezoids (like the task in figure 5.1, page 105), other polygons, and circles can be examined. Take a moment to consider the area task in figure 5.15.

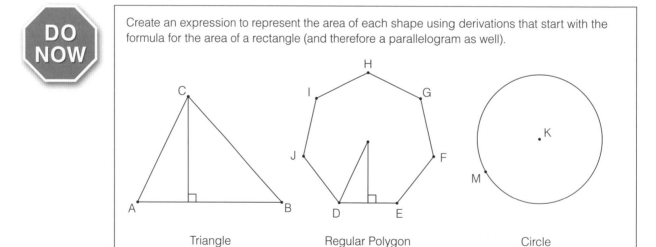

Figure 5.15: Area of triangle, polygon, and circle task.

How did you go about finding the area of each of these shapes? Examine the triangle first. How can this triangle be related to a parallelogram? If you were to rotate this triangle 180° about the midpoint of $\overline{BC}$, what would happen? Think back to the task in figure 5.1 (page 105) when the trapezoid was rotated to create a parallelogram. Figure 5.16 shows what happens to the pre-image and image when this rotation occurs.

What happens when you rotate this triangle 180°? When the original triangle is rotated and the pre-image and image are considered together, a parallelogram is created. The rotated triangle is labeled based on the correspondence to the vertices of the pre-image. The point A' is the rotated location of A in the image. This is a way to clearly describe the effect of the rotation on the pre-image. Due to the rotation, the point C could also be labeled B' and the point B could also be labeled C'; however, relabeling these points is not necessary for this exploration. The area of the parallelogram is the base

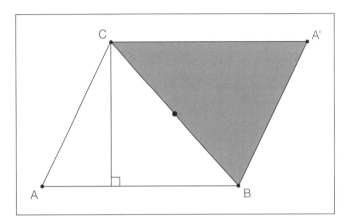

Figure 5.16: Rotation of triangle *ABC*.

times the height of the parallelogram. If you consider the base of the parallelogram to be $\overline{AB}$, then the height of the parallelogram would be the perpendicular distance from point C to that base. This is the same as the height of the original triangle. Since the area of the parallelogram would be the base times the height and the parallelogram is made up of two identical triangles, the original triangle would be half the area of the parallelogram, or $A_{tri} = \frac{1}{2}bh$. This is true whether the original triangle is acute, obtuse, or right. The triangle explored in this discussion was acute; composite shapes from obtuse and right triangles are shown in figure 5.17.

In all three cases in figures 5.16 and 5.17, the triangle is half of a parallelogram, so the formula for the area of a triangle would be $A_{tri} = \frac{1}{2}bh$.

Now that the area formula for the triangle has been derived, it can be applied to an exploration of regular polygons. A regular polygon has all sides equal in length *and* all angles equal in measure. How can you deter-

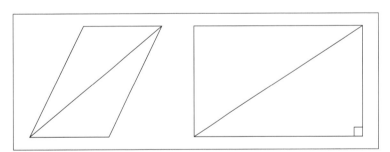

Figure 5.17: Obtuse triangle and right triangle compositions.

mine a generalized formula for the area of regular polygons? How can the polygon be decomposed into shapes for which you can find the area? Depending on the polygon, this may vary. For example, a regular hexagon could be decomposed into two trapezoids. A regular pentagon can be decomposed into a trapezoid and a triangle (see figure 5.18, page 116).

Since regular polygons have congruent sides and each vertex of the polygon is the same distance from the center of the shape, *all* regular polygons can be decomposed into a set of congruent triangles as shown

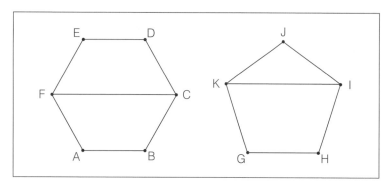

Figure 5.18: Decomposing a hexagon and a pentagon.

in figure 5.19 for the heptagon (a polygon with seven sides) from figure 5.15 (page 114).

How can you use this decomposition to generate a formula for the area of this regular heptagon? Since each of these triangles is congruent, you can find the area of one of the triangles and then multiply by seven. How would you generalize this idea to any regular polygon? For any regular polygon, the number of congruent triangles will match the number of sides of the polygon. The area of one triangle can be found with the base of the triangle, which is also a side of the polygon, and the height of the triangle. Thus, the area of a regular polygon would be $A_{reg\ poly}$ = ½shn, where s is the length of a side of the polygon, h is the height of the triangle, and n is the number of sides of the polygon.

Later, in high school geometry, students will learn that the height of this triangle is called the *apothem* of the polygon, abbreviated a. As the number of sides multiplied by the length of each side is the perimeter of the polygon (p), the area of a regular polygon is found with the formula $A_{reg\ poly}$ = ½ap. Students in high school make sense of this formula by drawing on their experiences from the middle grades of finding areas of regular polygons by decomposing the polygon into triangles.

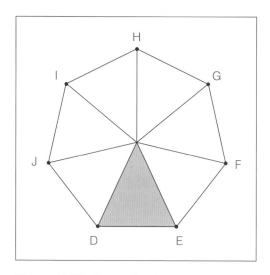

Figure 5.19: A regular heptagon decomposed into seven congruent triangles.

Now consider the circle from figure 5.15 (page 114). This shape creates more of a challenge, because as there are no straight sides in a circle, the properties of polygons cannot be used directly. Perimeter and area are found in different ways with circles. The perimeter of, or distance around, the circle is called the *circumference* and is determined by multiplying the diameter of the circle by π. The area of a circle, while less straightforward than the area of a trapezoid or triangle, can also be connected to the area of a parallelogram.

What would happen if you took the circle and cut it into small sectors using cuts like those you might use when cutting a pie or pizza? As the circle is decomposed into these slices, and the slices are rearranged as shown in figure 5.20, the shape begins to resemble a parallelogram. How can this be used to find the area of the circle? What are the dimensions of this new shape in terms of the parallelogram it approximates? What is the base of this parallelogram? If you examine the original circle, half of the pieces are oriented in one direction and the other half of the pieces are oriented in the opposite direction. This leaves half of the circumference of the circle on the "bottom" of the parallelogram (as shown in figure 5.20) and half of the circumference on the "top" of the parallelogram. Since the formula for the circumference of the circle is π times the diameter, the base of the parallelogram would

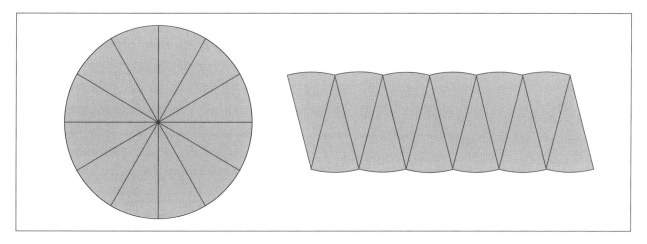

Figure 5.20: A circle decomposed.

be ½πd. What is the height of the parallelogram? The height of the parallelogram is the radius of the circle, or r. When the area of the parallelogram is found, the area of the circle then becomes A_{cir} = ½πdr = ½π$(2r)r$ = πr^2.

When students make sense of area formulas of different shapes, they begin to see the formulas as a connected and coherent system. This will allow students to solve real-world problems, which may include a variety of shapes composed together, as in the pool-deck problem in the video discussed later in this chapter. This coherent system is also applied to surface area.

Exploring Surface Area

Some three-dimensional objects are made up of faces—two-dimensional shapes that comprise the surface of the object. In the case of prisms and pyramids, the faces are polygons. Figure 5.21 provides an example of each. The bases of these objects are shown by shaded faces.

For prisms, there are always two bases that are identical polygons and in parallel planes to each other. In right prisms (prisms where the bases are perpendicular to the other faces), the other faces are rectangles. What would the shapes of the faces be for nonright prisms? Would any of the faces be rectangles? The answer is yes, but for which nonright prisms and which sides? This is an interesting investigation for students who need more challenge during mathematics instruction. For nonright prisms, the faces that connect the bases will be either rectangles or parallelograms that are not rectangles. For pyramids, one face will be the base (which could be any polygon) and the other faces are triangles, which meet at a point called the *apex*. A right pyramid has the apex directly over the center of the base. For this chapter, the prisms and pyramids explored will be right prisms and right pyramids.

What would happen if you completely covered all of the faces of a prism or pyramid with wrapping paper so there is no overlapping paper? How

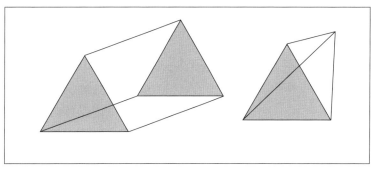

Figure 5.21: A triangular prism (left) and a triangular pyramid (right).

much wrapping paper would you need to use? This context provides a way for you to think about the surface area of the prism or pyramid. How can the area of all of the surfaces be determined? The surface area can be found by determining the area of each face and adding those areas together. If you take the faces and put them together into one shape so that they can be folded to make the prism or pyramid, you have made a composite shape called a *net* of the solid. The area of this net is the surface area of the prism or pyramid. Consider the nets in figure 5.22.

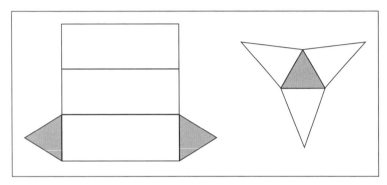

Figure 5.22: Nets for the triangular prism and triangular pyramid from figure 5.21.

How can a formula for surface area be generalized to any right prism or any right pyramid? Let's examine the prism first. The shaded triangles in the net of the prism in figure 5.22 are the bases of the prism. The other faces are known as *lateral faces*. These faces are all rectangles because the prism is a right prism. How are the dimensions of these rectangles related to the dimensions of the prism? How are the heights of the rectangles related to each other? The heights of the rectangles are all the same and represent the height of the prism, which is the distance between the bases of the prism. How do the lengths of the bases of the rectangles relate to the dimensions of the prism? Imagine the net in figure 5.22 folding to wrap around the prism in figure 5.21. Each rectangle is associated with one side of the base of the prism. What happens when you put the three rectangles together? What is the base of this composed rectangle? Imagine wrapping the composed rectangle around the prism; the base of this larger rectangle would connect to the base of the prism, so the length of this composed rectangle is the same as the perimeter of the triangle. The height of the composed rectangle is the height of the prism. What would happen if the base was a different polygon? This connection between the lateral faces and the base of the prism holds true for all right prisms, so the surface area of a right prism can be found using the formula $SA_{prism} = ph + 2B$ where p is the perimeter of the base, h is the height of the prism, and B is the area of the base (an uppercase B is used to distinguish B as a measure of area rather than b as a measure of length).

A similar strategy can be used to find the formula for the surface area of a right pyramid. With pyramids, there is only one base and the lateral faces are triangles. How does this change the formula for surface area? How does the perimeter of the base connect to the formula for the surface area of a pyramid? The bases of the triangles are the sides of the base of the pyramid. What is the height of the triangles? Is it the height of the pyramid? The height of the triangles is known as the *slant height* of the pyramid, since it is the height on the outside, or slanted side, of the pyramid. This is different from the height of the pyramid, or the distance from the vertex point, or apex, to the base of the pyramid. Similar to the prism, if you add the lateral faces together, you will get triangles whose bases total the perimeter of the base of the pyramid and whose height is the slant height of the right pyramid. Therefore, when the base of the pyramid is a regular polygon, the surface area of the right pyramid can be found using the formula $SA_{pyr} = \frac{1}{2}pl + B$ where p is the perimeter of the base, l is the slant height of the pyramid, and B is the area of the base of the pyramid. Why is this formula limited to right pyramids where the base is a regular polygon? When the base is not a regular polygon, the slant height of each triangle may be different, and the lateral faces will need to be calculated individually. Why does the formula include a factor of ½? The lateral faces are triangles, so they are half of the associated parallelograms. Why is the area of the base (B) not multiplied by 2 in this formula? That is because there is only one base in the pyramid.

Investigating Volume

Volume is another attribute of three-dimensional solids. Volume describes the number of cubic units an object can hold. Consider a rectangular prism. If you filled the prism with one layer of centimeter cubes, how many cubes would fill this layer? The layer would have the same number of cubes as the area of the base; in the case of a right rectangular prism, length times width of the rectangular base (see figure 5.23).

If these layers were then continually added until the prism was filled, there would be layers equal to the height of the prism. How could you determine the number of cubes that would fill the prism? The number of cubes that would fill the prism would be the product of the dimensions of the prism, often stated as $V_{rect\ prism} = lwh$. How can this be gen-

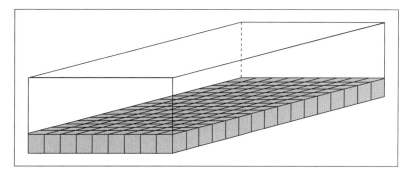

Figure 5.23: A rectangular prism with one layer filled.

eralized to a prism with any shaped base? This formula can be generalized to $V_{prism} = Bh$ where B is the area of the base and h is the height of the prism. This representation of the formula is made more evident by exploring volume as layering the cubes that cover the base of the prism, regardless of the shape of the base. It is helpful to begin the exploration with rectangular prisms because the volume of the first layer is easier to see because of the ability to fill it with whole cubic units.

How can you use knowledge of the volume of a prism to determine the volume of a pyramid? How are pyramids and prisms related? Consider a prism and a pyramid that have the same base and height (see figure 5.24). How are their volumes related?

If you filled the pyramid with water and poured it into the prism, how high do you think it would fill the prism? Figure 5.25 (page 120) shows a pyramid and its related prism after water from a full pyramid has been poured into the prism one time.

The contents of one pyramid fill the prism ⅓ full. Therefore, the volume of a prism is three times the volume of a pyramid with the same area of the base and height, so $V_{pyr} = \frac{1}{3}Bh$.

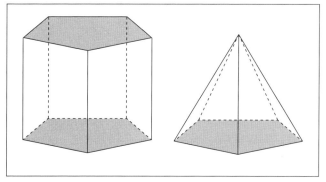

Figure 5.24: Prism and pyramid with the same base and same height.

The processes involved in developing formulas for area, surface area, and volume provide opportunities to engage students in Mathematical Practice 7, "Look for and make use of structure," as they connect the structures of shapes to each other. When students apply these formulas to make sense

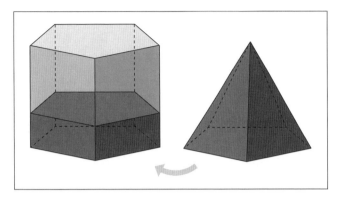

Figure 5.25: Contents of a pyramid poured into a prism.

of solving contextual problems that apply area, surface area, and volume concepts, they engage in Mathematical Practice 4, "Model with mathematics." Throughout middle-grades mathematics, as students explore and make sense of area, surface area, and volume of various shapes, context problems become more complex to include additional shapes that students must decompose. Success with these sorts of problems is improved when students are able to visualize the decompositions. Visualization is also used when exploring transformations.

Using Transformational Geometry

As students transition from grades 6–8 into high school, transformations are incorporated not only in the geometry curriculum, but in algebra as well. Transformations include four main types: (1) reflections, (2) translations, (3) rotations, and (4) dilations. Each transformation impacts shapes in different ways. Transformations are used to examine ideas of congruency and similarity as well as scale factor in meaningful ways.

Consider the transformations task in figure 5.26. You may want to make a copy of the diagrams in figure 5.26 before proceeding. For each transformation, use the pre-image and your understanding of the transformation to draw the location of the image.

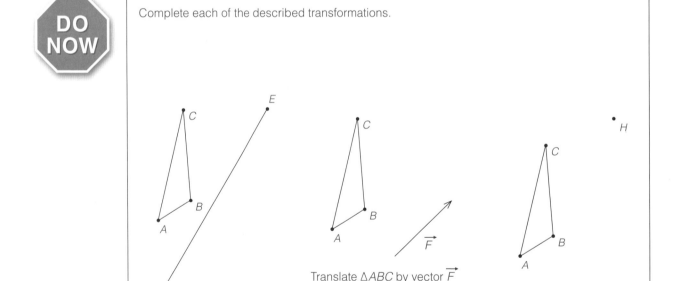

Complete each of the described transformations.

Reflect △ABC about $\overline{DE}$

Translate △ABC by vector $\vec{F}$

Rotate △ABC 45° clockwise about point H

Figure 5.26: Reflection, translation, and rotation of a triangle task.

*Visit **go.solution-tree.com/mathematics** for a free reproducible version of this figure.*

How did you determine the locations of the images? What properties are important to consider? With which transformation were you most comfortable? Did any of them create a challenge for you?

A reflection is like using a mirror. An object is reflected about a line, and the line becomes an axis of symmetry for the pre-image to the image. Every part of the pre-image (Δ*ABC*) on one side of the line of reflection ($\overline{DE}$) is on the opposite side of the line of reflection in the image (Δ*A'B'C'*) (see figure 5.27).

What do you notice about the pre-image and the image? Are they congruent or similar? What do you notice about their orientation? In the case of a reflection, the orientation is reversed, but the pre-image and image are congruent shapes. What is the same and what is different between the pre-image and the image? Every point in the image is the same perpendicular distance from $\overline{DE}$ as its corresponding point in the pre-image. Notice how the line of reflection is not vertical or horizontal. This helps you think about how to maintain the distance between the line of reflection and both the pre-image and the image in a meaningful way. In practice, maintaining this distance can be accomplished by folding a paper on the line of reflection to determine where the image appears.

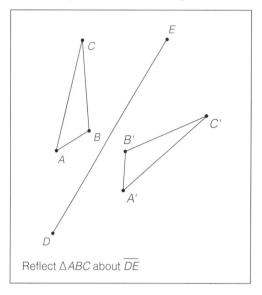

Reflect Δ*ABC* about $\overline{DE}$

Figure 5.27: Reflection of Δ*ABC*.

A translation occurs when the pre-image is moved with a given distance, direction, and angle, sometimes referred to as a *vector*. Every part of the pre-image is moved the same distance and in the same direction to create the corresponding part of the image (see figure 5.28).

What do you notice about the pre-image and the image with a translation? Are they congruent or similar? What do you notice about their orientation? In the case of a translation, the pre-image and image are congruent shapes and the orientation is maintained. The position in space has changed, but nothing else. This can be found in practice by copying the vector and using it to map the pre-image to the image.

A rotation occurs when the pre-image turns about a particular point in space using a particular angle. This point could be located on or within the original shape or outside the shape, but it must be a fixed point (see figure 5.29, page 122).

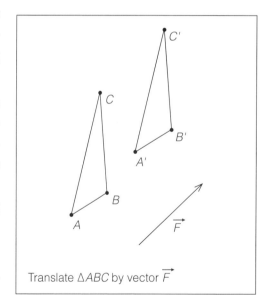

Translate Δ*ABC* by vector $\overrightarrow{F}$

Figure 5.28: Translation of Δ*ABC*.

What do you notice about the pre-image and the image with a rotation? Are they congruent or similar? What about their orientation? In the case of a rotation, the position is changed based on the angle of rotation and the location of the center of rotation. The pre-image and image, however, are congruent shapes. The pre-image has turned about the center of rotation

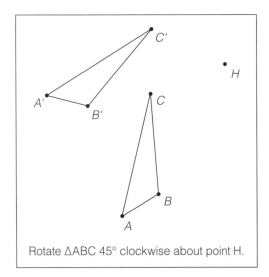

Rotate △ABC 45° clockwise about point H.

Figure 5.29: Rotation of △ABC.

to determine the image. How can you determine where the points of the image will appear? The measure of ∠CHC' is 45°, with a clockwise rotation. This tells you that points A' and B' will fall on the rays that would create 45° angles as ∠AHA' and ∠BHB'. Students will sometimes encounter a challenge when the center of rotation is separate from the shape, as in this case. It is important for students to consider how the shape rotates about the center and maintains the size and shape of the figure as well as the distance between the shape and the center of rotation.

These three transformations connect to congruency in that they are rigid motion transformations. They maintain the original pre-image, so the image is identical to the pre-image in size and shape. In all three cases illustrated in figures 5.27, 5.28, and 5.29, the result of the transformation preserves the original size and shape of the figure, although not necessarily the orientation. As students engage with geometric transformations, they use rigid motion transformations to show that shapes are congruent to each other. Students must be able to justify which transformation or combination of transformations would map the original figure onto the congruent shape.

While these first three types of transformations preserve the original shape, the transformation of dilation does not create a congruent shape. Instead, it creates a shape that is similar to the original shape—the same shape but drawn to a different scale (see figure 5.30). The *center of dilation* determines the direction of the transformation, and the *scale factor* determines the size of the image after dilation; together they determine the location of the image.

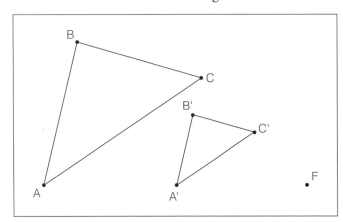

Figure 5.30: Dilation of △ABC with a scale factor of ½ to create △A'B'C'.

To determine the location of the image of △ABC relative to the pre-image with a scale of ½, construct line segments so that one endpoint of each line segment is a vertex of △ABC and the other endpoint is point F. Since the scale factor is ½, you should find the midpoint of each of these segments to determine the location of the vertices for the image A'B'C'. The vertices of the image lie halfway between the vertices of the pre-image and the center of dilation, so the sides of the image are ½ the length of the sides of the pre-image. This creates two similar triangles. In this case, the image is smaller than the pre-image because the scale factor is less than one.

If the scale factor is greater than one, then the vertices will create an image that is larger than the pre-image. Consider a dilation of **Δ***ABC* with a scale factor of two and the center of dilation at *F*. Instead of finding the midpoints of the segments connecting the vertices of **Δ***ABC* to *F*, you would construct three rays with *F* as the endpoint passing through the vertices of **Δ***ABC*. As the scale factor is two, the distance from the center of dilation to the transformed vertices would be twice the distance between the center of dilation and their corresponding vertices. The transformed vertices would be on the rays formed by the center of dilation and the vertices of the pre-image. The length of the sides of the image would be twice the length of the sides of **Δ***ABC*. The use of dilations and similarity connects to ratio and proportional reasoning in the middle grades (see chapter 2).

As you examined transformations and drew conclusions about what is maintained and what is changed from pre-image to image, you were engaged in Mathematical Practice 7, "Look for and make use of structure." Students should be able to make conjectures and apply understandings of the properties of transformations to identify an unknown transformation. Students also use transformations to prove geometric properties like congruence and similarity.

Relating Angles and Parallel Lines

Middle-grades geometry also includes an examination of types of angles within triangles and those formed by parallel lines and transversals. Students examine general types of angles, including supplementary, complementary, adjacent, and vertical angles. Supplementary and complementary angles can be adjacent angles or nonadjacent angles. Consider the task in figure 5.31.

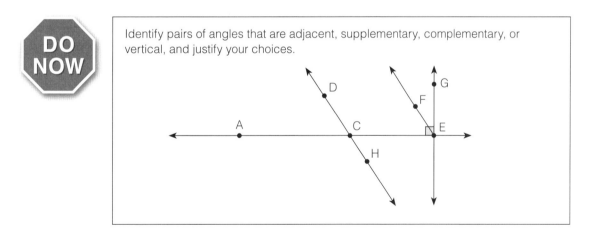

Figure 5.31: Identify supplementary, complementary, adjacent, and vertical angles.

How did you determine how to classify the angles? Classification involves understanding the definition of each angle type and applying that definition to make sense of which angles are which type. This is probably something you can do without much thought. However, *justifying* the relationships may be more challenging. In this diagram, for example, ∠*ACD* and ∠*DCE* are adjacent and supplementary. They share $\overrightarrow{CD}$. When placed side by side with no overlaps, they create a straight line, so their measures add to 180°. Similarly, ∠*CEF* and ∠*FEG* are adjacent and complementary since they share $\overrightarrow{EF}$, and, when placed side by side with no overlaps, they create lines that are perpendicular as the measures of the identified angles add to 90°. Since $\overleftrightarrow{AE}$ and $\overleftrightarrow{DH}$ intersect at point C, $\angle ACD$ and $\angle ECH$ are vertical angles.

How do the measures of $\angle ACD$ and $\angle ECH$ compare to each other? They are the same measure. Will this always be true? Could you prove it? You could measure angles formed by intersecting lines and use repeated reasoning to conclude that vertical angles always have the same measure, but this would not be a proof of the general case, only a conjecture based on the examples you tested. How could you use expressions and equations to help you? Since $\angle ACD$ and $\angle DCE$ are supplementary, $m\angle ACD + m\angle DCE = 180$. Similarly, $\angle DCE$ and $\angle ECH$ are supplementary, so $m\angle DCE + m\angle ECH = 180$. Using properties of equations, you can say $m\angle ACD + m\angle DCE = m\angle DCE + m\angle ECH$. Using aspects of solving equations from chapter 3, you can subtract $m\angle DCE$ from each side of the equation and you find that the vertical angles, $\angle ACD$ and $\angle ECH$, have the same measure. How can you use transformations to help you prove it? What happens if $\angle ACD$ is rotated 180° around point C? Consider copying the diagram onto a separate paper and rotating this angle. You will find that the image of $\angle ACD$ matches $\angle ECH$. These types of angle relationships are emphasized in the middle grades with respect to geometric concepts, and students are expected to use these relationships to prove other properties and to solve problems.

Consider the parallel lines cut by a transversal task in figure 5.32.

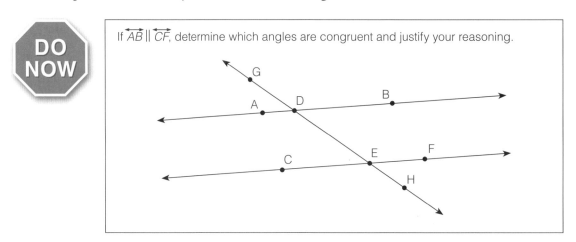

Figure 5.32: Parallel lines cut by a transversal task.

*Visit **go.solution-tree.com/mathematics** for a free reproducible version of this figure.*

Which angles did you determine to be congruent? How do you know? When lines are parallel like $\overleftrightarrow{AB}$ and $\overleftrightarrow{CF}$, different pairs of angles are formed when a transversal line, like $\overleftrightarrow{GH}$, intersects both parallel lines. As already discussed, vertical angles are congruent. There are four pairs of vertical angles in the diagram. They are $\angle ADG$ and $\angle BDE$, $\angle ADE$ and $\angle BDG$, $\angle DEC$ and $\angle HEF$, and $\angle DEF$ and $\angle ECH$. In addition, when parallel lines are cut by a transversal, special angle pairs that are congruent or supplementary are formed.

Trace the diagram in figure 5.32 two times on separate sheets of paper. What happens if you translate $\angle ADG$ along the vector $\overrightarrow{DE}$? What angles match this angle? The translated image of $\angle ADG$ is now concurrent with $\angle CED$, so they are congruent. They are called *corresponding angles* since they are located in corresponding locations relative to each parallel line. There are four pairs of corresponding angles in this diagram.

Now consider ∠*ADE*. You can see that ∠*ADE* and ∠*CEH* are corresponding angles, therefore they are congruent. What other angles are congruent to ∠*ADE*? For corresponding angles, you used a translation. What would happen if you used a rotation instead? Using your two tracings, where is the center of rotation and what angle is necessary to transform the image of ∠*ADE* to another angle in the diagram? You may have found that ∠*ADE* and ∠*FED* are also congruent. Where was your center of rotation, and what angle did you use to rotate? You should have found the center of rotation to be the midpoint of $\overline{DE}$ and the angle of rotation to be 180°. Are these corresponding angles? Do they lie in the same corresponding location? Not in this diagram. These angles are both between the parallel lines, so they are known as interior angles. They are on alternating sides of the transversal and thus called *alternate interior angles*. There is also one more pair of alternate interior angles.

Are these alternate interior angles always congruent? How can you use what you know about angle pairs to prove this? You know that ∠*ADE* is congruent to ∠*BDG* because they are vertical angles and ∠*BDG* is congruent to ∠*FED* because they are corresponding angles. Therefore, by using the transitive property, ∠*ADE* has the same measure as ∠*FED*. A similar justification can be made for *alternate exterior angles* (those that are on opposite sides of the transversal but on the outside of the parallel lines). Can you identify two pairs of alternate exterior angles? How are these angles related, and why? One pair of alternate exterior angles is ∠*GDB* and ∠*HEC*, and a second pair is ∠*GDA* and ∠*HEF*. Each pair of angles is congruent, through a similar reasoning process as described for alternate interior angles.

Another type of angle pair formed with parallel lines cut by a transversal is known as *same side interior angles*. Which angle pair do you think would be considered same side interior angles? In this case, they are on the same side of the transversal and between the two parallel lines. ∠*ADE* and ∠*CED* are same side interior angles. So are ∠*BDE* and ∠*FED*. Examining figure 5.32, how are same side interior angles related? Are they congruent? No. They are, in fact, supplementary. How can you justify this conclusion? How might you use transformations? How can you use corresponding angles and alternate interior angles to help you? Because ∠*ADE* and ∠*CEH* are corresponding angles, one can be translated to match the other. How are ∠*CEH* and ∠*CED* related? They are supplementary angles. Because ∠*ADE* ≅ ∠*CEH* and ∠*CEH* and ∠*CED* are supplementary, then ∠*ADE* and ∠*CED* must be supplementary as well. Same side interior angles can also be congruent if the transversal is perpendicular to the parallel lines so that each angle measures 90°.

As students explore these types of relationships, Mathematical Practice 5, "Use appropriate tools strategically," can be emphasized through the use of various tools to make sense of parallel lines and transversals. Students can use tracing or patty paper, transparencies, or the application of dynamic geometry environments (DGEs). Tracing paper and transparencies can be used to see how one angle can match another angle much like you did in the task in figure 5.32. There are a number of different DGEs from which to choose. The advantage of any DGE is the ability for students to examine patterns in a dynamic environment with precision and to see a large number of examples and relationships in a short period of time.

Consider the task in figure 5.32. If this task was given to students, they might use protractors to measure angles to determine relationships between angles, or they might use transparencies to copy the angles and use transformations to map them onto another angle. To truly be convinced, students would likely measure angles with a variety of examples of parallel lines cut by transversals. Students may draw faulty conclusions or fail to see an accurate conclusion because of inaccurate drawings or measurement tools. In a DGE, however, students could move the points and lines and see a variety of lines cut by transversals. The lines can be constructed to be parallel, and measurements are determined by technology, so precision is built into the environment. Through these environments, students can examine patterns and engage in Mathematical Practice 8, "Look for and express regularity in repeated reasoning." The focus of instruction is on examining patterns rather than just using a tool to measure, and the students are connecting the measurements to the patterns.

Proving the Pythagorean Theorem

The Pythagorean theorem is an important aspect of geometry that students can use to make sense of distance when it cannot be easily determined vertically or horizontally relative to the coordinate plane. The Pythagorean theorem applies only to right triangles and uses a relationship of the areas of squares drawn to each side of a right triangle (see figure 5.33).

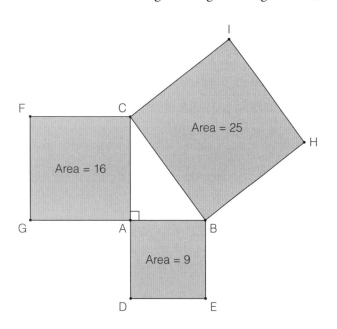

Figure 5.33: Areas of squares created from the sides of right triangle *ABC*.

How are the areas of the squares related? Is this always true? Draw additional right triangles on a grid paper. Do the areas of the squares drawn to each side match your conclusion for this triangle? For any right triangle, the sum of the areas of the squares drawn based on the lengths of the legs, or shorter sides of the right triangle, is equal to the area of the square based on the length of the hypotenuse, or longest side, of the right triangle. In figure 5.33, $\overline{AB}$ and $\overline{AC}$ are the legs, while $\overline{CB}$ is the hypotenuse. The area of the square drawn to side $\overline{AB}$ is nine square units, and the area of the square drawn to side $\overline{AC}$ is sixteen square units. The sum of these squares is twenty-five square units, which is the same as the area of the square drawn to side $\overline{CB}$. This can be written algebraically as $(leg\ 1)^2 + (leg\ 2)^2 = (hypotenuse)^2$ or $(AB)^2 + (AC)^2 = (BC)^2$. This is commonly written as $a^2 + b^2 = c^2$ where a and b are the lengths of the legs of the right triangle and c is the length of the hypotenuse. You can use a DGE or drawing on grid paper to convince yourself that this relationship is true, but why is it true? How can you prove the Pythagorean theorem?

In the middle grades, students need to be able to explain a proof of the Pythagorean theorem. There are several visual proofs of the Pythagorean theorem that use algebraic properties and relationships that students can explore in grades 6–8. Consider the visual proofs in figure 5.34 and determine how each leads to the relationship of $a^2 + b^2 = c^2$ and the Pythagorean theorem.

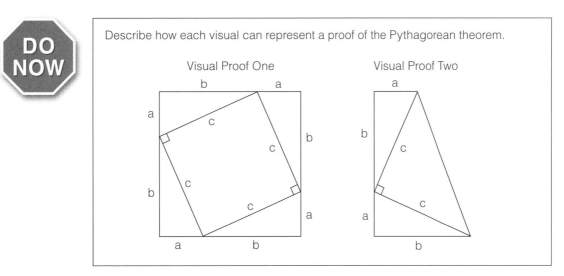

Figure 5.34: Representations to prove the Pythagorean theorem.

As you examine these two shapes, how can you use them to show the Pythagorean theorem is always true? There are no numerical values in these shapes, so the proof is generalizable to any values that fit the relationship of the sides of a right triangle. In both cases, the area of the large shape is decomposed into smaller shapes, and the area of the decomposed shapes can be used to show that the Pythagorean theorem holds (see figure 5.35).

Proof One	Proof Two
4 congruent triangles + 1 square	2 smaller congruent triangles + 1 larger triangle
= large square	= 1 trapezoid
$4(\frac{1}{2}ab) + c^2 = (a + b)^2$	$2(\frac{1}{2}ab) + \frac{1}{2}c \cdot c = \frac{1}{2}(a + b)(a + b)$
$2ab + c^2 = (a + b)(a + b)$	$\frac{1}{2}[2ab + c^2] = \frac{1}{2}(a + b)(a + b)$
$2ab + c^2 = a^2 + 2ab + b^2$	$2ab + c^2 = (a + b)(a + b)$
$c^2 = a^2 + b^2$	$2ab + c^2 = a^2 + 2ab + b^2$
	$c^2 = a^2 + b^2$

Figure 5.35: Algebraic proofs of the Pythagorean theorem.

The Pythagorean theorem can be proven through both geometric and algebraic means. As students explore measurement and geometry in grades 6–8, they engage in mathematical practices including sense making and justifying mathematical solutions and generalizations. Throughout middle-grades mathematics, students are finding generalized formulas for area, surface area, and volume and using those formulas to solve problems. Additionally, geometric properties, including transformations, angles, and the Pythagorean theorem, are examined with applications and connections to other areas of mathematics, including proportional reasoning as well as expressions and equations.

The Classroom

Throughout this chapter, you have explored your own thinking related to measurement and geometry. Now turn your attention to explore the classroom environment. The following videos provide insight into how measurement and geometry concepts can be developed with students in the classroom. The first video examines decomposing shapes to find area. In this video, students are presented with a task involving finding the area of tile surrounding a swimming pool. Before proceeding, solve the task in figure 5.36.

You are encouraged to watch the video in its entirety before proceeding.

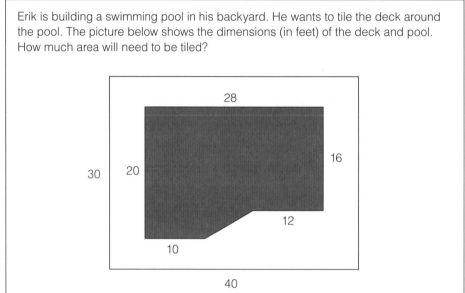

Erik is building a swimming pool in his backyard. He wants to tile the deck around the pool. The picture below shows the dimensions (in feet) of the deck and pool. How much area will need to be tiled?

Figure 5.36: Erik's pool deck tiling problem.

www.solution-tree.com/Finding_Area_in_Context

After viewing this video, what are your thoughts? What did you notice?

Perhaps you noticed that the teacher provides the task and gives students an opportunity to make sense of it prior to determining a solution, using the layer of facilitation "I facilitate the whole class." It is important to give students ample time to make sense of the task before working toward a solution. As students are asked to make sense of the task, they begin to make sense of methods for approaching solving the task. One student even begins to explain a method she might use. It is important in this case to be sure that all students understand what area is being found. Once this is established, students are given time to determine an answer and the teacher shifts to facilitating small groups of students. Does the teacher tell the students how to solve the problem? Does she tell the students how to decompose the pool in order to find the area? Notice how the teacher poses the problem and provides time for the students to explore solutions. She is more concerned with how students are making sense of the problem than following a particular strategy.

As the students work to find the area of the pool, notice how they decompose shapes to determine the area. Do the students all decompose the shape in the same way? The students do not all use the same method to make sense of the task. Some students even change their decomposition method as they realize one method is more efficient than another. It is important for students to see that one method may be more efficient than another, but that doesn't make either method incorrect. Take, for instance, the notion explored in this video of dividing the pool into a rectangle and a trapezoid. When first mentioned, two students interpret this differently. One draws a horizontal line to make a rectangle with a trapezoid below while the other draws vertical lines to create a trapezoid between two rectangles. As these students explore finding the area, the second student changes his method to the first student's method. Notice the teacher asks specifically why he changed his method. What does he say? Note that the first method is not wrong but that the second method is easier to determine the dimensions. He begins to recognize that some methods are more efficient than others.

The teacher encourages students to engage in Mathematical Practice 1, "Make sense of problems and persevere in solving them," and Mathematical Practice 2, "Reason abstractly and quantitatively." As students determine the area of the pool, they have meaningful discussions regarding different ways to decompose the shape and make sense of the problem and how to solve it. Additionally, they connect their knowledge of finding area to a real-world context with finding the area that would be tiled around the swimming pool. They use the context to make sense of the problem and then make sense of the answer in light of the context. This even applies to the units for the answer. Recall that a numerical answer is not sufficient. When a student provides the answer of 700 without a unit, the unit is asked for and a brief discussion ensues as to the appropriate unit. This requires students to return to the context and use it to determine that square feet is the appropriate unit of measure.

In the next video, high school students are engaged in making sense of rotations about a center of rotation. We encourage you to watch the video in its entirety before proceeding.

www.solution-tree.com/Visualizing_Rotations

After viewing this video, what did you notice? What were the students doing to engage in the task? In this case, the task is given and students conjecture the placement of the image of the flag after a rotation. They then use transparencies to verify if their conjecture is correct. The students use tools such as markers and protractors, and they discuss common mistakes they made in their conjectures. They determine the important aspects of the rotation, both the angle and the direction. One student provides a conjecture that the stick of the flag should be at the center of rotation, providing an opportunity for the teacher to address a misconception. What happens then? Most students believe the base of the flag should be at the center of rotation, and others disagree. Instead of providing an answer to this, the teacher asks the students who disagree to support their reasoning. This is an important aspect of classroom discourse that helps lead the class to conclusions that are founded in mathematical reasoning and that they can justify. Students use other transformations to help them justify that the center of rotation could be outside the shape being rotated. Students conclude that the distance from the pre-image to the center of rotation should be maintained.

TQE Process

At this point, it may be helpful to watch the first video (page 128) again, paying particular attention to the tasks, questioning, and opportunities to collect evidence of student learning. The TQE process can help you frame your observations. Teachers who have a deep understanding of the mathematics they teach:

- Select appropriate *tasks* to support identified learning goals
- Facilitate productive *questioning* during instruction to engage students in Mathematical Practices
- Collect and use student *evidence* in the formative assessment process during instruction

The *task* chosen for this lesson involves decomposition of shapes in order to determine the area. One of the first teacher moves is setting up the task. The teacher provides time for the students to make sense of the task. This is important as the students need to make sense of the problem for themselves. The teacher could have told the students they needed to find the area of the pool and subtract it from the largest rectangle in order to find the area of the deck, but that would not have helped the students to make sense of the task for themselves. The construction of the task is important to ensure that the shape could easily be decomposed in a variety of ways. It is designed so that there are multiple solution paths, an important aspect to consider when choosing and implementing tasks in the classroom.

Notice how the teacher uses *questioning* as a way to promote classroom discourse and foster understanding. What happens when a student doesn't answer the question asked? The teacher asks the class if they have any questions about the problem, and the student begins to provide a method for solving it. How does the teacher handle this situation? She helps the class see that the student is providing a solution method and asks another student to explain what the first student meant. Asking questions like "What did she say?" provides impetus for other students to make sense of the problem and of alternate solution methods.

As the teacher is circulating to different groups and asking questions, she is gathering *evidence* of their learning. She asks questions to elicit students' thinking and support their productive talk. She uses a formative assessment process to determine how students are making sense of the concepts. The evidence gathered helps determine what strategies she may want to have students explain and in what order. As the students explain their thinking in the whole-class discussion, the focus shifts back to the student who had earlier provided one method for dividing up the pool. He changed his method to match another student's explanation. The teacher capitalizes on this shift and asks the student, "Why did you change? Why did you use her technique?" With his response of "It was easier to find the numbers," issues of efficiency are highlighted. By asking, "Who did it differently?" a variety of solution methods are encouraged, allowing multiple students to provide evidence of their learning. Even though the first method is possibly the most efficient, the class discussion continues to show that other methods are viable.

The Response

Typical areas of difficulty related to measurement and geometry stem from making assumptions and applying geometric relationships incorrectly. Students may misapply a formula or use incorrect values within formulas. In most cases, this stems from students having memorized a formula without understanding why that formula works. Many students, for example, will forget to multiply by ½ when finding the area of a triangle. This is less likely to happen if students have had opportunities to explore derivations of the formula for the area of a triangle and how it is related to other shapes. While students who understand that a triangle is half of a parallelogram are less likely to make this error, when they do, this gentle reminder is all they need. For students who have simply memorized a formula, this relationship does not make sense, so it is easy to forget. In this case, it becomes necessary to provide students experiences to examine why the area of a triangle is multiplied by ½. These experiences could include context-based problems, as well as composing and decomposing shapes to make sense of the formula. The same pattern emerges with the formula for the volume of a pyramid. When students understand the relationship that one prism is filled with three pyramids having the same base and height as the prism, the factor of ⅓ makes sense, so it is less likely to be left out of the calculation. When providing intervention for students who have only memorized formulas, it is important to go back to the derivation and help students make sense of why the formulas work and where they come from. This may include providing manipulatives and tools for students to use to make sense of these formulas and why they are appropriate for the given shape.

Also related to geometric measurement, many students confuse base and height with length and width in parallelograms and triangles. Students want to use any two dimensions of a parallelogram or a triangle as the base and height. For right triangles and rectangles, this can be effective and efficient; however, for acute or obtuse triangles and parallelograms that are not rectangles, the height may be a different measure than the width. Providing experiences for students to see the difference between height and width becomes critical for students to avoid this misconception from the beginning and to intervene with students who have developed this misconception.

Finally, a common error students make with respect to geometry is incorrectly applying properties. Students assume that properties hold for all shapes, and sometimes, this is related to a lack of precision during instruction. If students always hear "$a^2 + b^2 = c^2$," without hearing a specific reference to a right triangle, students will assume this is true for the sides of all triangles and not just right triangles. Similar conclusions can be made regarding angles formed by parallel lines compared to nonparallel lines. As much as students need to engage in Mathematical Practice 6, "Attend to precision," so do teachers. Often, teachers know that a property only applies to a particular situation, but they neglect to reinforce that with their students. This creates misconceptions, particularly with students who struggle and tend to search for a trick to make a problem easier. Interventions should focus on making sense of the mathematics, not rote memorization or tricks to make the procedures easier to remember. These tricks and procedures are often forgotten or misapplied because there was a lack of understanding to connect to the trick or procedure.

Reflections

1. What do you feel are the key points in this chapter?

2. What challenges might you face when implementing the key ideas from this chapter? How will you overcome them?

3. What are the important features for developing an understanding of measurement and geometry, and how will you ensure your instruction embeds the support needed for these features?

4. Select a recent lesson you have taught or observed focused on measurement or geometry. Relate this lesson to the TQE process.

5. What changes will you make to your planning and instruction based on what you read and considered from this chapter?

Reflections

CHAPTER 6

Statistics and Probability

How do you define statistics and probability? Statistics is the collection, analysis, and interpretation of data, often in numeric form. Probability involves examining the fraction of successful outcomes out of the total number of possible outcomes and is an important factor in understanding random processes. This chapter explores how to build conceptual understanding of statistics and probability in the middle grades. You will reason with problem-solving situations that involve statistical investigations, data analysis, and probability.

The Challenge

One important aspect of statistical reasoning in the middle grades is comparing data sets. What are the different ways that you can compare data sets? How do you know which way to use for particular data sets? Think about your answers to these questions as you complete the task shown in figure 6.1.

Mr. Richard and Ms. Chutto decide to compare the grades in their two science classes on the last quiz.

The grades in Mr. Richard's class on the twenty-point quiz were:

| 14 | 15 | 17 | 16 | 11 | 11 | 15 | 12 | 16 | 20 | 14 | 15 |
| 17 | 13 | 17 | 15 | 11 | 14 | 15 | 17 | 20 | 16 | 14 | |

The grades in Ms. Chutto's class on the twenty-point quiz were:

| 17 | 18 | 16 | 17 | 14 | 15 | 14 | 17 | 20 | 18 | 20 | 13 |
| 17 | 18 | 15 | 17 | 20 | 17 | 15 | 17 | 18 | 18 | 20 | |

Whose class did better on the quiz? How do you know?

Figure 6.1: Comparing data sets.

How did you decide to compare the two data sets? If you used a measure to compare, what measure did you choose? If you used a display to compare, what display did you use? These choices are important and should be based on the characteristics of the data, as your choices of measure and display can affect the analysis and comparison of the data sets.

Perhaps you thought about measures of center, like mean, median, or mode. If so, how did you determine which measure of center to use? Did you base the measure you chose on the structure of the data set, or did you find all of the measures and pick the one that looked best? Your choice of a measure of center should be based on which value provides the best summary of the data set. For example, if the data are distributed evenly, without large gaps between data points, then the mean may be the best choice to summarize a data set. If the data have extreme values, called outliers, then the median may be the best choice. The mode is used very rarely as a measure of center, only for data sets that have values that occur far more often than other elements in the data set.

Now, examine the data sets to think about which measure would be best. A dot plot is one way to examine the distribution of a data set to help determine which measure of center to use (see figure 6.2).

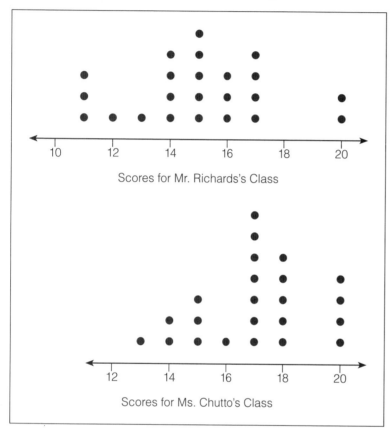

Figure 6.2: Dot plots for Mr. Richards's and Ms. Chutto's classes of quiz scores.

Notice that the data in both dot plots are somewhat balanced. While the data are not completely symmetrical, they are balanced enough that either mean or median can be used as a representation of each set of data. There is no value that occurs far more often than any other, so the mode would not be an appropriate choice to describe the data set. In this case, the mean or the median would be the better choice for analysis. Often in statistics, if either of these measures of center can be used, you use the mean, because its calculation includes every element in the data set.

How do you interpret the mean? The mean for Mr. Richard's class is 15 and for Ms. Chutto's class is 17. Conceptually, the mean can be considered as the balancing point of a data set, creating a measure of center that includes the impact of every single data element. You can think about the mean as regrouping the scores and making everyone have the same score. In this case, there are 23 scores. If you add all 23 scores together, you have the total score for all 23 students. Why, then, would you divide by 23 to find the mean? If you take the total of these scores and give all 23 students the same score, you are dividing the total points into 23 new, and equal, groups.

How is the median different from the mean? Interestingly, for these two data sets, the median for each class has the same numerical value as the mean for each class, 15 and 17 respectively. What does that tell you about the data? When the mean and the median are the same value, the data set probably does not have extreme values. When there is an extreme value in the data set, the mean may be shifted toward that value, but the median is less affected by the extreme value. For example, in Mr. Richards's class, if one of the lowest scores of 11 was changed to zero, the mean would be reduced, but the median would remain the same. Remember, you want the measure of center to represent the entire data set, not be influenced by a few elements in the data set. So, if there are elements that will inappropriately skew the measure of center when used in a calculation, the median may be the best choice.

Dot plots provide a visual representation of the shape, center, and spread of a data set (see figure 6.2). If you imagine a bar surrounding each vertical set of dots, the shape of the data can be seen by examining the relationship between the heights of the bars. How would you describe the shape of the data for each of these classes? In thinking about the shape of the data, you might ask yourself questions such as:

- Are the bars about the same height? If they are, then the data represent a uniform distribution.

- Are the bars of the dot plot taller in the center? If they are, then the data represent a bell-shaped curve (sometimes called a *normal curve*).

- Are there clusters of relatively tall bars about the same height? If so, then the data represent either bimodal (if there are two peaks) or multimodal (multiple peaks) distributions, where there are groupings of data elements around certain values.

- Are the bars taller on one side of the plot than the other? If so, then the data represent a skewed distribution (see figure 6.3).

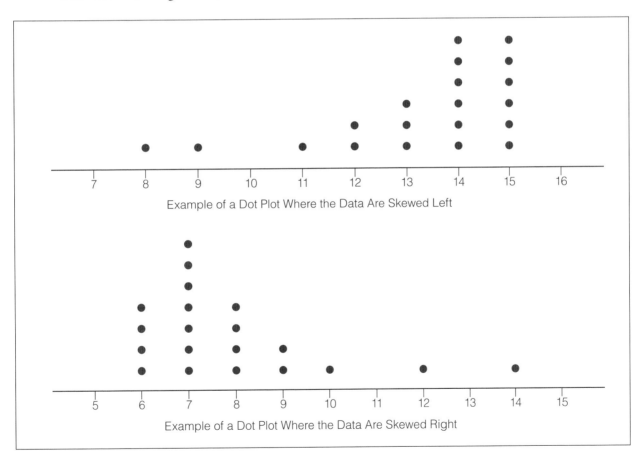

Figure 6.3: Examples of skewed data.

The spread of the data is a reference to how the data extend across the range of the data set. Why is the spread important to consider? Take, for example, Mr. Richards's scores. It might be helpful for Mr. Richards to consider the spread of his data to notice that there was a spike in the number of scores at the lowest value, 11, while the other peaks hovered between scores of 14 and 17. Compare this to Ms. Chutto's spread where more students scored at 17 and higher.

How can this spread of data be quantified? This is where measures of variability come in to play. In the initial development of statistical reasoning, you might explore the mean absolute deviation (MAD), a numerical representation that finds the mean of the distances between the mean of the data set and each individual element. For example, in Mr. Richards's data set (see figure 6.1, page 133), the distance between the first value (14) and the mean (15) is one; the distance between the second element (15) and the mean of the data set is zero; the distance between the third element (17) and the mean of the data set is two. Note, because you focus on distance, the value is always positive, and hence the reference is to *absolute* deviation, a connection to absolute value. Continuing this process for each element in the data set allows you to find the difference, or deviation, between each of the data elements and the mean of the data set. Once you have this collection of differences, you find the mean of them to determine the MAD. This measure provides one way to consider the spread of the data, or how far the data elements are from the mean. For Mr. Richards's set of scores, the MAD is approximately 1.83 and for Ms. Chutto's set of scores, the MAD is about 1.48. These values for MAD indicate that the spread of these two data sets is close, however, the spread of the scores in Ms. Chutto's class is less than the spread of scores in Mr. Richards's class.

Another way to measure the spread of a data set is by what is called the *interquartile range*. The interquartile range is a measure determined by the relationship of the data elements that are between the 25th percentile and 75th percentile of a given data set. What is meant by *percentile*, and how is it related to *percentage*? The percentile tells you the value below which a given percentage of the data set lies.

For example, if the score at the 25th percentile is 12, then 25 percent of the data points are at or below a score of 12. This measure is often connected with a *box plot*. Box plots—sometimes called box and whisker plots—display data by showing the location of the quartiles, which are the boundaries for splitting the data up into fourths (or *quartiles*). In order to determine the quartiles, first you determine the median. Next, find the median value of all data elements less than the overall median (this is termed the *lower quartile*) and then determine the median of all of the data elements greater than the overall median (this is termed the *upper quartile*). The difference between the upper quartile and the lower quartile is the interquartile range and demonstrates the range of possible values of the middle 50 percent of the data set. As the interquartile range examines the middle 50 percent of the data set, it is less affected by what occurs in the smaller and larger values of the data set. The general sense of the spread of the data from the median can be elicited by examining the width of each quartile in the box plot (see figure 6.4).

For Mr. Richards's data set, the interquartile range is three (17 – 14). For Ms. Chutto's data set, the interquartile range is also three (18 – 15). This is another way to show that the spread of each of these two data sets is very close.

The last way to discuss spread of the data is the range, the difference between the greatest and least value in a data set. The range for Mr. Richards's set of scores is nine, and the range for Ms. Chutto's set of scores is seven. This can also be seen in the box plot as the total length of the box plot (see figure 6.4).

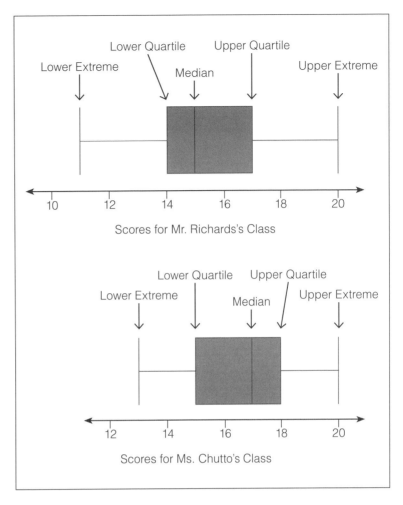

Figure 6.4: Box plots for Mr. Richards's and Ms. Chutto's sets of scores.

What are the advantages of choosing a dot plot instead of a box plot to display the data? The dot plot shows each element in the data set, which is helpful when you want to see the distribution of scores of the basketball team over the year and look for patterns in the data, for example. The box plot shows five representative points of the data set, based on the quartiles of the data. This type of display can be helpful to compare data sets of different sizes, such as having mathematics scores from two teachers who have different numbers of students in their classes. It is important to think about the best data display to use based on the information you have and the questions you are trying to answer.

In this example, you see how one aspect of the development of statistical understanding in the middle grades explores measures of center and variation and how to effectively use those measures to compare data sets. A comparison should not be just a listing of different measures but rather an analysis of which measures to use as well as an understanding of the reasons to justify their selection. The selection of the appropriate display, as well as the appropriate measure of center or variability, demonstrates the importance of Mathematical Practice 5, "Use appropriate tools strategically." In this case, the tool is the choice of measure and display.

The Progression

Statistics and probability in the middle grades begin with the investigation of statistical questions, such as "How did your class do on the last quiz?" Students move from thinking about an individual data point (for example, one quiz score) to reasoning about a group of data points (for example, the quiz scores for an entire class). When expanding the investigation to include multiple quiz scores, you begin to think about how statistics, such as measures of center and variation, can be used to make sense of the situation.

The progression of developing understanding in statistics and probability begins with learning to interpret statistical questions and using the tools of analysis with single variable data sets. As students progress through the middle grades, they move from single variable to two-variable data sets. Underlying these statistical concepts is how randomness can have an impact on real-world events. Randomness is a link between statistics and probability in the middle grades. Students learn to make inferences based on the rules of probability. Combining the ideas of data analysis, probability, and randomness provides the foundation for statistical reasoning in the middle grades, as the following progression shows.

- Make sense of statistical questions.

- Describe and compare data sets by using shape, center, and spread.

- Display data sets using histograms and box plots.

- Determine the role of context when interpreting a data set.

- Construct and interpret scatterplots.

- Generalize and infer about a population based on information from a sample.

- Create probability models to represent real-world events.

- Design and use simulations of real-world events.

- Examine frequencies and relative frequencies in two-way tables.

Grade 6

In the elementary grades, students created line (or dot) plots, picture graphs, and bar graphs. In the middle grades, students build on these tools to create histograms and box plots. This extension—along with the measures of center and variation—allows students to analyze, display, and describe data sets by shape, center, and spread. An important development that begins in sixth grade is the understanding that a statistical question requires variation in the possible responses.

Grade 7

In seventh grade, students compare two data sets, using measures of center and variation. They make inferences about the differences between given data sets. Students also begin to build their understanding of probability by exploring chance, sample spaces, and basic probability models. Probability models include connections to equally and unequally likely events, and students simulate real-world events. Students make connections between long-run relative frequency and both experimental and theoretical probability models.

Randomness is investigated as a strategy to create a representative sample from a larger population. Students learn how randomness plays an important role in determining the validity of an inference. They consider how sampling can create variation within statistical results and how statistical measures of a sample differ from parameters of a population. The impact of variation in the random sampling process, sample size, and the taking of multiple samples from a population are also considered.

Grade 8

Eighth-grade students begin to investigate relationships between two variables. This co-variation is explored in two ways—through the creation and interpretation of scatterplots and through the relationships expressed in two-way tables. Scatterplots are constructed, and students examine the relationship between the variables represented on the graph, looking at lines that fit the data informally, saving more precise methods for later study in high school. Students also make sense of the relationship between two variables by building and interpreting two-way tables. Students use frequencies and relative frequencies to describe the pattern of association between two variables and think about how closely related the variables are to one another.

The Mathematics

The study of statistics and probability provides an excellent opportunity to connect to students' lives regarding the decisions they make on a daily basis. Understanding how data are collected and analyzed helps middle-grades students become critical consumers of the information they come across every day. For example, interpreting the results of a survey is impacted by who did or did not respond. Making an interpretation from the analysis of a box plot or scatterplot is affected by how representative the data are of the population in question. Some of the topics with which students in grades 6–8 engage include designing statistical investigations, simulating real-world events, creating and interpreting scatterplots, and investigating two-way tables.

Engaging in Statistical Investigations

Statistical investigations provide the opportunity to predict what may happen in the future. What should be taken into consideration as you develop a statistical investigation? You should begin with what question you want to answer, ensuring that the question is statistical in nature (questions that include the possibility of variation in the responses). Next, you need to plan the investigation, thinking about how you will collect the data so that they represent who or what should be considered in a fair way. This allows the results to be termed *valid*. You next collect your data and then analyze the data to answer the question of your investigation. An example of this type of investigation can be seen in figure 6.5.

 Harvey is conducting a survey of seventh-grade students to determine what they feel are the most important characteristics in a best friend. He knows that there are 300 students in the seventh grade at his school. Design a statistical investigation that would allow him to determine a reasonable estimate for what seventh-grade students feel are the most important characteristics in a best friend.

Figure 6.5: Designing a statistical investigation.

What would you include in your design so that Harvey is able to gain valid information that will allow him to accurately predict the feelings of all of the seventh-grade students at his school? How will your design determine who should participate in Harvey's survey? One design you may have considered is for Harvey to include everyone in the seventh grade in his survey. This would be called a *census test*, as it would include the entire population of interest, which in this case is all students in the seventh grade.

While this would provide an accurate prediction of the outcome (in fact, it would not be a prediction, but rather the choice of the entire population), it would be challenging and cumbersome to administer the survey to all 300 students. For this reason, your design should indicate that a part of the entire population should complete the survey. This group would be a *sample* of the overall population. But how do you select the participants? You need to try to get a representative sample. A *representative sample* includes people who have ideas, thoughts, backgrounds, and other characteristics proportional to the population of interest, so that you can make the best possible prediction about how the population would think.

In the case of Harvey's survey, if he wants to get a representative sample, he should not just ask a few of his friends, but rather he should select seventh-grade students who would be representative of the entire population of seventh-grade students. What are ways that Harvey could decide who to ask to complete his questionnaire, which is the set of questions that Harvey asks in his survey? One way to create a sample that should be representative is to select participants randomly. *Random selection* occurs when every member of a population has an equal chance of being included and the choice of inclusion is made in a fair manner. How can you create a random sample? Your design may include putting every seventh-grade student's name into a large container, mixing them up, and selecting a certain number of names to participate. You may also use a random number generator to select enough students to include in the survey.

How many students should be selected to complete the questionnaire? In the middle grades, the procedure for determining an appropriate number of participants is not deeply investigated, but rather, a *reasonable* number is expected for your plan. Surveying only a few students would not be enough. A number around 30 (about 10 percent of the population) might be seen as the smallest appropriate sample size for this population, with the understanding that the more participants you include, the better the predictions you can make from the data. While random selection cannot guarantee a representative sample, it does tend to produce samples with characteristics similar to the overall population, and this design will often lead to valid inferences.

Simulating Real-World Events

You can also use statistical reasoning to simulate real-world events. Students can experience simulation in many different ways. One example of a simulation is modeling how prizes are won in a contest as described in figure 6.6.

Chen's favorite restaurant is having a contest. Any customer who gets a full set of four different cards will win a free meal every week for a year! You get a randomly selected card each time you eat at the restaurant. Chen finds out the cards are distributed in the following manner: 50% of all of the cards are Card 1, 30% are Card 2, 15% are Card 3, and 5% are Card 4. Design a simulation that will predict how many times Chen needs to eat at his favorite restaurant before he wins the prize.

Figure 6.6: Simulating winning a prize task.

How will you design a simulation to model this task? How will you weight the outcomes so that the balance is correct based on the availability of cards? In thinking about how to simulate this real-world event, you have to consider a probability model that will: (1) allow for the outcomes to be weighted in the manner written in the task and (2) include how the event occurs in context. One way to weight the outcomes would be to assign numbers to model the distribution of each card and use a random number generator (such as a table of random numbers, a calculator, an online website, or an app). You need to assign 50 percent of the possibilities as Card 1, 30 percent as Card 2, and so on. Similarly, you must select the random number generator to correspond to the distribution. How could you do this? You could use a random number generator using the numbers 1–20, with 1–10 as Card 1 (50 percent of the numbers), 11–16 as Card 2 (30 percent of the numbers), 17–19 as Card 3 (15 percent of the numbers), and 20 as Card 4 (5 percent of the numbers). You could also decide to have 20 cards as a representative sample of the cards in the task and let 10 cards represent Card 1, 6 cards represent Card 2, 3 cards represent Card 3, and 1 card represent Card 4. How does this distribution of cards match the situation presented? The key in representing the scenario is that the percentages contained within the simulation tool (in this case, the cards) are the same as in the scenario.

The next step is to define what represents a visit to the restaurant, and you probably decided that one selection of the simulation tool is one visit to the restaurant. To model the scenario, you select from your simulation tool until you have a representation for each type of card. If you use cards, you need to be sure to replace the card and randomize them before the next selection; otherwise, the percentage changes throughout your simulation.

You could run a simulation using the random number generator in figure 6.7. Starting with the top left and reading down, you would get Card 1 (2), Card 2 (12), Card 1 (1), Card 1 (10), Card 3 (19), and so on. You would need to keep counting the number of visits until you have one of each card, which happens on visit 22; you get Card 4 on the 22nd visit. Based on this simulation, Chen would need to eat at the restaurant 22 times to earn the prize of free meals for a year.

Do you believe that this is the correct answer to the problem? Will Chen automatically win if he goes to the restaurant 22 times? Try a little experiment. Instead of starting with the first entry on the leftmost column, try starting with the second column and read down. What number of visits do you determine when you start at this point on the randomly generated list? You start with 14 (Card 2), then get 20 (Card 4), 7 (Card 1), and keep going until you get Card 3 with a 19 on the 18th visit. If you choose another starting point, you may get a different answer. This is important in understanding statistical reasoning, variability, and simulation. Answers will be different with different attempts, and predicting actual events is often very difficult to do. These understandings lead to creating mathematical representations that demonstrate how randomness can be used to model real-world events, an example of Mathematical Practice 4, "Model with mathematics."

2	14	20	10	18
12	20	17	17	15
1	7	16	8	1
10	4	6	20	10
19	2	19	20	11
15	9	18	4	16
3	2	4	15	8
10	16	4	18	15
17	10	16	3	4
15	7	20	5	8
18	8	14	7	17
2	1	15	14	7
13	3	2	1	11
5	8	12	20	6
18	13	4	4	3
17	9	5	1	19
8	13	19	12	1
7	19	10	17	6
19	3	7	14	11
11	1	5	4	17

Source: List generated at random.org.

Figure 6.7: Random numbers.

Creating and Interpreting Scatterplots

Students undergo an important transition in their development of statistical reasoning when they build from analyzing one variable to analyzing the relationship between two variables. One way to explore the relationship between two variables is through the use of a scatterplot. The task in figure 6.8 provides an opportunity to create a scatterplot based on a data set.

Heather collected data on the height and arm span of students in her mathematics class. She collected the following information (all the measurements are in centimeters).

Create a scatterplot of the given data, and describe the relationship between student height and arm span.

Height	Arm Span
150	147
153	145
162	161
162	150
158	158
172	178
140	162
176	156
166	172
151	157
160	152
155	155
150	150
178	178
164	176
172	172
166	171
163	153
164	163
171	169
175	175

Figure 6.8: Scatterplot task.

How did you decide which variable was on which axis? It is typical to place the independent variable on the horizontal axis and the dependent variable on the vertical axis. However, for this example, you could choose to place either variable on the horizontal axis, as there is not a dependent relationship between the variables. How did you decide on the scales for the vertical and horizontal axes? Did you start your graph at 0, or did you start at 140 to match the data? Does it matter? You need to consider how your choice of data display is influenced by the context as well as how the display may influence your analysis. Your choice in the scales for your axes can influence how you make sense of the patterns in the data. Your data will feel more spread out if you start your scale at 140 and place a break in each scale rather than completing each scale starting from 0. Does your graph look like the one in figure 6.9?

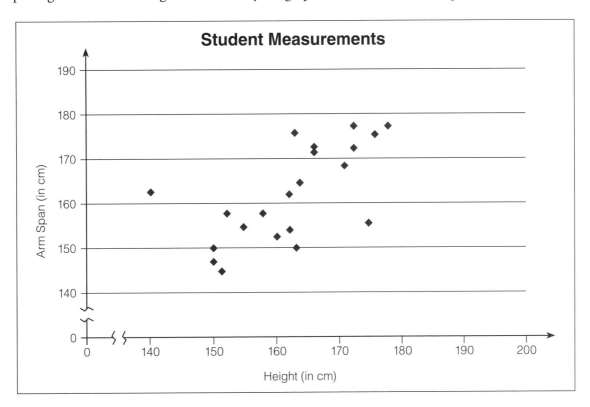

Figure 6.9: Scatterplot of student measurements.

How did you describe the relationship between the two variables? Think about how you can estimate the relationship between the measurements using the pattern you see in the data from the scatterplot. How can you describe a line on the graph to show the basic relationship? One way to describe the line would be to select two points that are representative of the data set and connect them with a line. If you drew a line that connected the ordered pairs (150, 150) and (178, 178), you would create the line $y = x$, showing that the basic relationship in the data is that a student's height is about the same as his or her arm span. What does the slope mean in this context? The slope represents the amount of change in a student's arm span based on a one-unit increase in his or her height, so there is a one-centimeter increase in arm span for every one-centimeter increase in height. You could adjust the line to create different fits. How does adjusting the line affect the interpretation of the slope? Is one representation of the line better than others? Is there one right answer? In the middle grades, there are only good fits to the data; students will explore best fit in high school (for a discussion of lines of best fit, see chapter 6 of *Making Sense of Teaching Mathematics in High School* [Nolan et al., 2016]). The key at this level is to look for and describe the pattern. The ability to move between graph and context and to make sense of the features of the linear trend and connect it to (or not connect it to) the context in this task are important demonstrations of Mathematical Practice 2, "Reason abstractly and quantitatively."

How would you use the line you determined to make predictions about a student's arm span if you knew his or her height? Would your prediction always be correct? This is where you extend your understanding of variability to know that while the prediction is generally correct, there will always be the possibility of variance; there may be a difference between your prediction and an actual value. In fact, you can see that variance in the collected data does not follow a perfectly linear pattern. Variance always plays a role in statistical reasoning, and understanding that role is an important factor in understanding how to model and predict real-world events.

While scatterplots can be used to explore some relationships involving two variables, another tool is a two-way table. You can use two-way tables to explore the relationships between two variables that are expressed as counts rather than continuous values.

Investigating Two-Way Tables

Two-way tables display summary data on two different categorical variables. They are organized in a way that allows you to compare them simultaneously. Consider the task in figure 6.10.

Sylvester asked all of the students in three health classes whether they prefer fruit or vegetables. He organized the information in the two-way table below. Determine answers to the questions below.

	Fruit	Vegetables	Total
Boys	25	30	55
Girls	20	10	30
Total	45	40	85

Do girls like fruit or vegetables better? Who likes fruit more, girls or boys? How do you know? What is the probability that one of the surveyed students likes fruit better than vegetables? What is the probability that a boy likes fruit more than vegetables?

Figure 6.10: Two-way table task.

How does the two-way table help you make sense of the problem? In what ways might students need to engage in Mathematical Practice 6, "Attend to precision," as they respond to this task? It is very important that students are careful with reading both the questions and the table when using two-way tables. Based on the information in this table, girls prefer fruit instead of vegetables 20 to 10 (or 66⅔ percent to 33⅓ percent if you prefer percent). For the question of who likes fruit more, although more boys like fruit than girls (25 to 20), the percentage of boys who like fruit is slightly greater than 45 percent (25 out of 55) while the percent of girls who like fruit is 66⅔ percent, so you should conclude that girls like fruit better. This is an example of proportional reasoning embedded in probability concepts. The last two questions are designed to get you to think about the whole group, for which the probability of liking fruit is $^{45}/_{85}$, or about 53 percent, compared to the probability that a boy likes fruit, which is about 45 percent.

The ability to interpret a two-way table correctly stems from working to make sense of the information and how it is organized, in rows, in columns, and as part-to-part and part-to-whole relationships. This organization allows you to connect understandings from proportional reasoning, rational number representations, and statistical reasoning.

The Classroom

The videos for this chapter represent classroom examples of the same type of statistical reasoning that you experienced with your tasks. You will explore how students make sense of this reasoning in the middle grades and in high school. The first video engages sixth-grade students with a data set and its accompanying dot plot. Students begin the lesson by estimating the number of jelly beans in a jar as a way to consider measures of center and to connect to a data set they will analyze. You are encouraged to watch the video in its entirety before proceeding.

www.solution-tree.com/Determining_the_Appropriate_
Measure_of_Center

Having seen how the students work to make sense of the different measures of center, what are you thinking? How do the students engage with the task?

Asking students to determine their own estimate for the number of jelly beans in the container allows them to connect to the context by making their own conjectures. This provides the opportunity for all students to think about the context of the data set. In some lessons, students struggle to make sense of the activity because they fail to grasp the context in which the task is set. By providing this introduction to the task, all students experience how the data may have been collected and what the data set represents. This provides a common background for students so that everyone starts with an understanding of the context, which is achieved through the level of the layers of facilitation, "I facilitate the whole class."

Some students struggle to blend their personal experiences and views with analysis of the given data set. When asked for a number that would represent the entire data set, one student's response is 109, the smallest number in the given data set. His justification comes not from statistical reasoning using the data set, but rather in regard to the size of the container and his group's estimates. How would you address this response? The teacher does not identify the response as being incorrect, but rather identifies how the student determined his response based on his group's estimates.

The class next discusses the median and the mean as possible choices for a single value to represent the data set. Notice how the teacher asks questions of the students to have them provide the definitions of both median and mean, and shares with them the value for each measure. Notice how this ties in to the learning goal of analyzing the data set. The key here is not to calculate the median or the mean, but rather to have the students provide the definition of these terms and discuss the role of mean and median in representing this specific data set. With that in mind, the teacher chooses not to take time in this task to calculate the median or the mean, but rather to discuss how to determine these values and then provides them. This keeps the focus on the concepts instead of the procedures.

Next, the conversation focuses on why the mean and the median are different values. A student discusses how the differences in numbers in the data set can have an impact, and the teacher responds by asking the student for a specific number that appears to be different than the rest. While the term *outlier* is not a requirement for student understanding at this grade level, providing students information within the context of the lesson supports their understanding in later coursework. Near the end of the lesson, the teacher has a student connect his original estimate to the given data set, and the student links it to the concept of outlier.

In the second video, high school students are examining a two-way table and considering aspects of conditional probability. Watch this video before proceeding.

www.solution-tree.com/Interpreting_Two-Way
_Frequency_Tables

In this video, students are investigating a two-way table to determine if two different conditional probabilities are the same—the probability of having a job if you own a car and the probability of owning a car if you have a job. The two-way table is set up in a way that these two conditional probabilities are equal. What do you notice about how the students approach the task? How does the teacher encourage students to engage in the task?

The challenge for students is to see beyond the specific numbers and determine if the probabilities will be equal if the numbers are different. Notice how the groups discuss their thinking about the task. One group considers only the numbers in the table and makes their conclusions based on those numbers. Another group considers how if the numbers change, the relationships might be different and the two probabilities would not be the same. Notice how the questioning of the teacher moves from student to student in each group to determine if the students agree with one another. The teacher is seeing the degree to which the students are sharing their thinking and making sense of the problem. These students are engaging in Mathematical Practice 1, "Make sense of problems and persevere in solving them."

TQE Process

Now, it might be helpful to watch the first video (page 145) for a second time, paying close attention to the tasks, questioning, and opportunities to collect evidence of student learning. The TQE process can help you frame your observations. Teachers who have a deep understanding of the mathematics they teach:

- Select appropriate *tasks* to support identified learning goals

- Facilitate productive *questioning* during instruction to engage students in Mathematical Practices

- Collect and use student *evidence* in the formative assessment process during instruction

The *task* chosen for this lesson supports students to connect statistical concepts to real-world data. You might notice that the teacher is intentional about allowing the students to make sense of the task themselves. Initially, students discuss their own estimates. This allows them to make sense of the context in very personal ways. Once these estimates are made, the teacher facilitates the students to think about the learning goal by asking about having one number represent the group of estimates. The task directly supports the learning goal and was chosen to provide opportunities to compare the measures of central tendency and to introduce the link between these measures and the concept of outliers. This promotes productive talk among the students by helping them connect to the data on the dot plot. The teacher helps students stay engaged in the group conversation and helps students make sense of each other's work. He uses questions to guide students to consider which measure of center would be better for the given data set without telling the students the answers, thus using the task to support the learning goal.

Notice how the teacher uses *questioning* and the conversations in the class to assess how students are making sense of the task and of the mathematical content. He asks questions to determine if students understand the definition of both mean and median, and how to apply those meanings in the context of the task. He allows students to extend their thinking when the student states that his estimate of 40 would be an outlier of the given data set. When the first student offers the data element of 109 to represent the data set, the teacher guides the discussion to include other students and other ideas. In order to check that the first student learned about measures of central tendency during the lesson, the teacher returns to that student at the end of the lesson to check for understanding. Through strategic use of thinking questions and the selection of students to answer those questions, the teacher uses a formative assessment process to support the development of understanding.

The students provide *evidence* of their learning as they engage in the lesson. Students connect their own estimates to the estimates in the given data set. They begin by making sense of how the data are collected, individually and as a class, and then move to analyze a display of a different set of data. After they make sense of the given data, they link back to their estimates and integrate the two data sets together, demonstrating how one of their estimates would act as an outlier in the given data set. By reasoning with actual estimates as well as a given set of data, these students engage in Mathematical Practice 2, "Reason abstractly and quantitatively."

You are encouraged to take some time to reflect on your own teaching. In what ways can you allow students the time and opportunity to make sense of the concepts you are teaching? How can you engage your students in meaningful conversations with one another and establish the expectation that they work together to develop shared understanding of the concepts?

The Response

One of the key features of understanding statistical reasoning in grades 6–8 is the importance of basing answers on the given information, not on preconceived notions or personal experiences. For example, when a fair coin is flipped nine times and it lands on heads each time, many students will feel that there is a greater chance of landing on tails on the next flip. They feel that the law of averages will work in the favor of landing on tails rather than heads on the next coin flip. Instead of understanding that with a fair coin, there is always a 50 percent chance of heads as the outcome and a 50 percent chance of tails as the outcome, they believe that the coin has some type of memory of the past and will work to balance out results. While there is a statistical law of large numbers, which describes that, over time, experimental probability will get closer to theoretical probability, this relates to many trials and is not predictive of individual outcomes. Students who have sound statistical reasoning understand that individual events include random variability and that in true probabilistic events, the predictability of individual outcomes is consistent over time. It is important to provide students experiences working with data that may challenge their preconceived notions, to conduct statistical and probability experiments, and to address both their beliefs and their ability to use data to support their conclusions.

Another area where some students need support involves comparing data sets. Students need the tools and understandings to be able to make valid and important statistical comparisons within and between data sets. Students need exposure to many types of data sets to learn the reasons behind the choice of statistical measure and data display. It is important for students to select the measure and the type of display, and to be able to justify those choices. You need to be sure that students are making comparisons that are deep in nature and go beyond the superficial aspects of data. When comparing two data sets, students should demonstrate understanding of shape, center, and spread and how they relate to the importance of the data comparison. Students need to link the statistical analysis to the real-world event being modeled, or the value of statistical reasoning is lost. What does the difference in the measure or the sample size mean in comparing the two data sets? And what does it mean to the context of the problem? When students struggle to make connections between the data set and statistical measures, this could be an indication that students need interventions that include providing additional contexts and experiences that support understanding the statistical measures.

Students will understand statistical reasoning if they are given the opportunity to create and test conjectures and display and analyze their data in ways that are meaningful to them. Contexts need to be relevant to *students* in order to ensure that they engage in making sense of problems. You must provide students time to engage in that sense making rather than having them wait for you to provide the sense making for them.

Reflections

1. What do you feel are the key points in this chapter?

2. What challenges might you face when implementing the key ideas from this chapter? How will you overcome them?

3. What are the important features for developing an understanding of statistics and probability for students, and how will you ensure your instruction embeds the support needed for these features?

4. Select a recent lesson you have taught or observed focused on statistics or probability. Relate this lesson to the TQE process.

5. What changes will you make to your planning and instruction based on what you read and considered from this chapter?

EPILOGUE

Next Steps

An important role of mathematics teachers is to help students understand mathematics as a focused, coherent, and rigorous area of study, regardless of the specific content standards used. To teach mathematics with such depth, you must have a strong understanding of the mathematics yourself as well as a myriad of teaching strategies and tools with which to engage students. Hopefully, by providing the necessary knowledge, tools, and opportunities for you to become a *learner* of mathematics once more, this book has empowered you to fill this role.

Now what? How do you take what you learned from *doing* mathematics and make good use of it as the *teacher* of mathematics?

Our position is that you first need to apply what you learned to your lesson planning. Are you planning for instruction that focuses on teaching concepts before procedures? How is your planning aligned to developing learning progressions? How will you ensure that your lessons do not end up as a collection of activities? What follows are strategies that will help you use what you experienced as learners and apply it to what you do as teachers.

Focus on Content

At the heart of meaningful mathematics experiences is mathematics content. A focus on content addresses the *what* of mathematics instruction. What is the mathematical idea or concept you want students to develop and learn as a result of the lesson you facilitate? With your collaborative team, discuss the content that will best serve your students as you progress through the school year. Everything that happens in a mathematics lesson—every task, every activity, every question, every element of the formative assessment process—provides an opportunity to strengthen students' understanding of mathematics content. Thus, it is important for you and your team to engage in collaborative planning about the mathematics content of a unit before the unit begins. Having made sense of mathematics for teaching provides you with a focus on content that will help you and your students have more meaningful and productive experiences with mathematics.

Select Good Tasks

As you've seen throughout this book, your focus on content is revealed in the tasks you select for students to engage in during instruction, so be sure to address this element of instruction during planning. Good tasks are those that support students in learning meaningful mathematics (concepts and, when appropriate, procedures). Other byproducts of good tasks include students engaging in meaningful discourse, developing critical thinking, having multiple ways of representing their thinking (definitions, equations, drawings, and so on), and building fluency (choosing strategies that are most efficient for a given task) in mathematics.

Good tasks also support students in acquiring proficiency with the Mathematical Practices, thereby supporting students' development in mathematics that will last beyond their current grade of study. As you teach, you have the opportunity to engage in the formative assessment process through the use of good tasks. By selecting good tasks, you set the stage for your students to develop strong conceptual understandings of mathematics. We modeled this for you through the tasks provided in this book.

Align Instruction With the Progression of Mathematics

Knowing how mathematics progresses within and across grades is a valuable asset for planning mathematics lessons. As students develop mathematically, you want their classroom experiences to be aligned with how the mathematics should progress. These understandings are important in both planning and implementing instructional processes. In this book, we've facilitated the alignment of instruction with the progression of mathematics within and across grades.

Build Your Mathematics Content Knowledge

Throughout this book, we have addressed mathematics content that is meaningful for your grade band. We have also addressed the content from the perspective that teachers need to facilitate meaningful mathematics instruction. In each chapter, we encouraged you to engage with the mathematics for the purpose of building your mathematics content knowledge by doing mathematics. Our aim was to provide you the support you needed for your understanding of mathematics so that you could subsequently engage your students in similar ways.

Observe Other Teachers of Mathematics

Making Sense of Mathematics for Teaching Grades 6–8 has provided you the opportunity to observe mathematics teaching in action. Through videos and examples, you were able to see students engaged in meaningful mathematics based on rich tasks. We hope this provided an opportunity for you to nurture discourse within your collaborative teams about teaching and learning mathematics. For each video, our aim was to guide you to examine the teacher moves and student exchanges that support the students' learning of mathematics. We are confident that each video provides nuggets of insight and confirmation that will help you clarify your thinking about and improve your teaching of mathematics. We encourage you to continue this practice by observing your fellow teachers when possible and inviting them to observe you.

Respond Appropriately to Students' Struggles With Mathematics

Students' progress in mathematics is often met with some level of struggle with understanding mathematics concepts and applying procedures. Some students even struggle with the language (words, symbols, and so on) of mathematics. Some misunderstandings are unintentionally perpetuated when mathematics is not deeply understood by teachers (such as, subtracting always makes smaller, or multiplication always makes larger). By preparing for common misunderstandings and errors, you will be better able to help students successfully engage with mathematics and overcome barriers to understanding. Using the formative assessment process to determine what students know and do not know provides opportunities for you and your collaborative team to reflect together to improve instruction.

Now What?

How has *Making Sense of Mathematics for Teaching Grades 6–8* helped prepare you for your next steps? How will you use the TQE process to inform your practice?

- How will you select appropriate *tasks* to support identified learning goals?
- How will you facilitate productive *questioning* during instruction to engage students in Mathematical Practices?
- How will you collect and use student *evidence* in the formative assessment process during instruction?

In responding to these questions within your collaborative team, your focus should also include the four critical, guiding questions of the PLC (DuFour et al., 2010).

1. What do we want students to learn and be able to do?
2. How will we know if they know it?
3. How will we respond if they don't know it?
4. How will we respond if they do know it?

Now that you have reached the conclusion of this book, we also ask you to respond to these three questions in the spirit of continuing the reflective process.

1. What do you know now that you did not know before interacting with this book?
2. What do you still need to learn now that you have completed this book?
3. How will you obtain the knowledge you still need?

References

Ball, D. L., Thames, M. H., & Phelps, G. (2008). Content knowledge for teaching: What makes it special? *Journal of Teacher Education, 59*(5), 389–407.

Cramer, K., & Post, T. (1993). Connecting research to teaching proportional reasoning. *Mathematics Teacher, 86*(5), 404–407.

Dixon, J. K., Adams, T. L., & Nolan, E. C. (2015). *Beyond the Common Core: A handbook for mathematics in a PLC at Work, grades K–5.* T. D. Kanold (Ed.). Bloomington, IN: Solution Tree Press.

Dixon, J. K., Andreasen, J. B., Avila, C. L., Bawatneh, Z., Deichert, D. L., Howse, T. D., et al. (2014). Redefining the whole: Common errors in elementary preservice teachers' self-authored word problems for fraction subtraction. *Investigations in Mathematics Learning, 7*(1), 1–22.

Dixon, J. K., Andreasen, J. B., Roy, G. J., Wheeldon, D. A., & Tobias, J. M. (2011). Developing prospective teachers' productive disposition toward fraction operations. In D. J. Brahier & W. R. Speer (Eds.), *Motivation and disposition: Pathways to learning mathematics* (73rd NCTM Yearbook, pp. 279–289). Reston, VA: National Council of Teachers of Mathematics.

Dixon, J. K., Nolan, E. C., Adams, T. L., Tobias, J. M., & Barmoha, G. (2016). *Making sense of mathematics for teaching grades 3–5.* Bloomington, IN: Solution Tree Press.

DuFour, R., DuFour, R., Eaker, R., & Many, T. (2010). *Learning by doing: A handbook for Professional Learning Communities at Work* (2nd ed.). Bloomington, IN: Solution Tree Press.

Fisher, D., & Frey, N. (2003). Writing instruction for struggling adolescent readers: A gradual release model. *Journal of Adolescent and Adult Literacy, 46*(5), 396–405.

Karp, K. S., Bush, S. B., & Dougherty, B. J. (2014). 13 rules that expire. *Teaching Children Mathematics, 21*(1), 18–25.

Kilpatrick, J., Swafford, J., & Findell, B. (Eds.). (2001). *Adding it up: Helping children learn mathematics.* Washington, DC: National Academies Press.

Kisa, M. T., & Stein, M. K. (2015). Learning to see teaching in new ways: A foundation for maintaining cognitive demand. *American Educational Research Journal, 52*(1), 105–136.

National Council of Supervisors of Mathematics. (2014). *It's TIME: Themes and imperatives for mathematics education.* Bloomington, IN: Solution Tree Press.

National Council of Teachers of Mathematics. (2014). *Principles to actions: Ensuring mathematical success for all.* Reston, VA: Author.

National Governors Association Center for Best Practices & Council of Chief State School Officers. (2010). *Common Core State Standards for mathematics.* Washington, DC: Authors. Accessed at www.corestandards.org/assets/CCSSI_Math%20Standards.pdf on January 31, 2015.

Nolan, E. C., Dixon, J. K., Safi, F., & Haciomeroglu, E. S. (2016). *Making sense of mathematics for teaching high school*. Bloomington, IN: Solution Tree Press.

Stein, M. K., & Smith, M. S. (1998). Mathematical tasks as a framework for reflection: From research to practice. *Mathematics Teaching in the Middle School, 3*(4), 268–275.

Stephan, M. L. (2009). What are you worth? *Mathematics Teaching in the Middle School, 15*(1), 16–23.

Index

Beyond the Common Core series
Edited by Timothy D. Kanold
Designed to go well beyond the content of your state's standards, this series offers K–12 mathematics instructors and other educators in PLCs an action-oriented guide for focusing curriculum and assessments to positively impact student achievement.
BKF627, BKF628, BKF626, BKF634

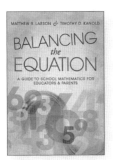

Balancing the Equation
By Matthew R. Larson and Timothy D. Kanold
This book focuses on educators and parents who seek to improve students' understanding and success in mathematics. The authors tackle misconceptions about mathematics education and draw on peer-reviewed research about the instructional elements that can significantly improve student learning.
BKF723

Engage in the Mathematical Practices
By Kit Norris and Sarah Schuhl
Discover more than 40 strategies for ensuring students learn critical reasoning skills and retain understanding. Each chapter is devoted to a different Standard for Mathematical Practice and offers an in-depth look at why the standard is important for students' understanding of mathematics. Grades K–5
BKF670

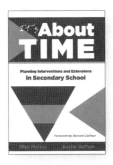

It's About Time, Secondary
Edited by Mike Mattos and Austin Buffum
Carve out effective intervention and extension time at all three tiers of the RTI pyramid. Explore more than a dozen examples of creative and flexible scheduling, and gain access to tools you can use immediately to overcome implementation challenges.
BKF610

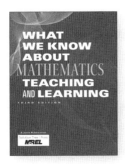

What We Know About Mathematics Teaching and Learning, Third Edition
By McREL
Designed for accessibility, this book supports mathematics education reform and brings the rich world of education research and practice to preK–12 educators. It asks important questions, provides background research, offers implications for improving classroom instruction, and lists resources for further reading.
BKF395

Solution Tree | Press   a division of
Solution Tree

Visit solution-tree.com or call 800.733.6786 to order.

DIG DEEP INTO CONTENT
DIXON · NOLAN · ADAMS
MATHEMATICS

Bring Dixon Nolan Adams Mathematics experts to your school

Juli K. Dixon

Edward C. Nolan

Thomasenia Lott Adams

Janet B. Andreasen
Guy Barmoha
Lisa Brooks
Kristopher Childs
Craig Cullen
Brian Dean

Lakesia L. Dupree
Jennifer Eli
Erhan Selcuk Haciomeroglu
Tashana Howse
Stephanie Luke
Amanda Miller

Samantha Neff
George J. Roy
Farshid Safi
Jennifer Tobias
Taylar Wenzel

Our Services

1. Big-Picture Shifts in Content and Instruction

Introduce content-based strategies to transform teaching and advance learning.

2. Content Institutes

Build the capacity of teachers on important concepts and learning progressions for grades K–2, 3–5, 6–8, and 9–12 based upon the *Making Sense of Mathematics for Teaching* series.

3. Implementation Workshops

Support teachers to apply new strategies gained from Service 2 into instruction using the ten high-leverage team actions from the *Beyond the Common Core* series.

4. On-Site Support

Discover how to unpack learning progressions within and across teacher teams; focus teacher observations and evaluations on moving mathematics instruction forward; and support implementation of a focused, coherent, and rigorous curriculum.

Evidence of Effectiveness

Pasco County School District | Land O' Lakes, FL

Demographics

- 4,937 Teachers
- 68,904 Students
- 52% Free and reduced lunch

Discovery Education Benchmark Assessments

Grade	EOY 2014 % DE	EOY 2015 % DE
2	49%	66%
3	59%	72%
4	63%	70%
5	62%	75%

"The River Ridge High School Geometry PLC went from ninth out of fourteen high schools in terms of Geometry EOC proficiency in 2013–2014 to first out of fourteen high schools in Pasco County, Florida, for the 2014–2015 school year."

—Katia Clouse, Geometry PLC leader, River Ridge High School, New Port Richey, Florida

Contact your local representative
888.409.1682